FOOLPROOF FRENCH COOKERY

RAYMOND BLANC

Step by step to
everyone's favourite
French recipes

Food photography by Jean Cazals

Published by BBC Worldwide Ltd,
Woodlands, 80 Wood Lane,
London W12 0TT

First published 2002
Copyright © Raymond Blanc 2002
The moral right of Raymond Blanc to be identified as the author of this work
has been asserted.

Food photography © Jean Cazals 2002

ISBN 0 563 53464 8

Commissioning editor: Vivien Bowler
Project editor: Sarah Lavelle
Copy editor: Jane Middleton
Art direction and design: Lisa Pettibone
Production controller: Susan Currie
Home economist: Marie Ange Lapierre
Stylist: Sue Rowlands

The publishers would like to thank Divertimenti and Summerill and Bishop
for their help in supplying items used in the photographs.

Set in Univers
Printed and bound in Italy by L.E.G.O. spa
Colour separations by Kestrel Digital Colour, Chelmsford

All the recipes in this book were cooked using a fan-assisted oven.
For conventional ovens, add 10°C (50°F) to the cooking temperature.

Contents

Introduction

These recipes demonstrate what is really good about French cuisine. The conviviality, the friends and laughter; the simple, hearty food, the rustic bread dipped into the sauce, and the heady red wine that will be drunk.

Most French life revolves around mealtimes, and my family was no exception. In France the table is still the centre of the house – not the bedroom, as many of my English guests might believe. The high priestess was my mother, whose creative force was born out of poverty, not wealth. She had to feed five children on a small budget, yet we ate like kings. For her, cooking was an act of love. At an early age, I was taught to love and respect food, for its beauty, its freshness and also its price. This simple philosophy has been a strong influence on my career as a chef.

The repertoire of French regional cuisine is almost inexhaustible. Even General de Gaulle, in a fit of Gallic temper, once protested, 'How can you govern a country that has 365 different cheeses and three times more regional dishes!'

Each of the recipes I have chosen is very expressive of my mother's cuisine. They are simple, rustic and completely delicious. They will grace your day-to-day table as much as a dinner party. I hope that they will give you as much joy as they have given me, as you share them with your family and friends.

The step-by-step photography will give you a real insight into how the dishes are created. This book will dispel the myth that French cuisine is difficult to master. Success will breed confidence, and shared enjoyment in the simple, creative act of cooking.

Ingredients and Equipment

INGREDIENTS

Butter (unsalted)

At last more and more British cooks are switching from salted to unsalted butter for cooking. Unsalted butter is better, as it contains fewer impurities and less whey – and, of course, there's no salt either. It can be heated to a much higher temperature without burning and its flavour will not interfere with the taste of the dish. The Normandy region is renowned for its butter and cream and it still produces some of the best in the world.

For serving, I very much like salted butter, especially the one with the flakes of salt trapped inside.

As for margarine, I simply never use it in my kitchen. It is a synthetic product that cannot compare with butter and, equally, we do not yet know the side effects of transfats (hydrogenated fats that make products more solid at room temperature).

Cheeses

If you are going to offer cheese to your guests at a dinner party, whether you choose to serve it after or before the dessert, offer a small selection of the best-quality farmhouse cheeses rather than a number of factory-produced ones.

Gruyère

This cow's milk cheese is one of the most famous in the world. It is native to my birth-place, Franche-Comté, which is the biggest producer of milk in France, and is such an important cheese that we have given it its own town – Poligny. Gruyère is slightly saltier than Emmenthal, with a firm, compact texture. Its melting qualities lend themselves perfectly to the creation of many dishes.

Roquefort

Roquefort is made from sheep's milk and is often looked upon as the best of blue cheeses. It comes from the southwest of France and is ripened in the damp caves under the village of Roquefort-sur-Soulzon. It is the quality of the milk, the processing of the curd and the addition of *Penicillium roqueforti* that give us this unique and remarkable cheese.

Chicken

For years we have been inundated with cheap, mass-produced, tasteless poultry. Unfortunately, this is still happening today, although it is becoming easier to find a better-quality bird. Always try to buy an organic or top-quality free range chicken – it is well worth it. There will have been no additives or antibiotics included in its diet, and it will have had space in which to run around and be a happy chicken. The result of this is that it will certainly taste better.

Above: chicory

Above: Roquefort (left) and Gruyère (right)

Chicory

Also known as Belgian endive, this is little used in salads in the UK, which is a shame as it has an excellent, crunchy texture and a delicate, bittersweet taste. The best dressings to accompany it are made with extra-virgin olive oil or walnut oil.

Cream

Crème fraîche is a traditional ingredient in French cooking. It has a distinctive sharp and lemony taste, which makes it the perfect accompaniment for any summer fruit. It also goes brilliantly well with soups or any dish that requires a degree of piquancy.

Whipping cream is the cream I use most for cooking. It whips and cooks very well and does not separate easily when boiled.

Duck fat

For many years, duck and goose fat have been used extensively in the southwest of France, particularly in Gascony in the Languedoc. From them, a new cooking technique was born – confit. Various cuts of meat or poultry are immersed in the fat and cooked at just under simmering point to give them the most succulent texture and flavour. Duck confit is one of the most celebrated French dishes.

Both duck and goose fat are monounsaturated, which means they can help to combat the bad effects of cholesterol; also the fat does not permeate the meat when you confit it.

Duck and goose fat can be found in some large supermarkets and delicatessens.

Eggs

Always try to buy organic or free range eggs, as they come from chickens that have been fed a more natural diet. Their taste will be so much better.

Five-spice powder

This classic combination of spices is indispensable to Oriental cooking and is also used in French cuisine. The spice blend is made up of equal quantities of finely ground anise, star anise, cinnamon, cloves and fennel seeds. Like all spices, it should be stored in a cool, dark place.

Garlic

My beloved garlic has always played centre stage in French regional cuisine. Because of its powerful aroma, I recommend that you cook it rather than eat it raw. Once cooked, its flesh becomes quite sweet and will lend character and layers of flavour to a dish.

The medicinal qualities of garlic are legendary. It is a medicine cabinet in its own right. Its virtues may explain what nutritionists call the French paradox – for centuries the French have made the table the centre of their home and the centre of their life; they have indulged their oral compulsions in every possible way. Yet they have a lower rate of fatal heart disease than any other Western country. Perhaps it is the wine as well?

Herbs

Herbs are used extensively in French cuisine. Always try to buy fresh ones, as they are now available everywhere and invariably have a livelier taste.

However, certain herbs do respond well to drying. These are rosemary, sage, thyme, bay, oregano, marjoram and verbena. When using dried herbs, use half the recommended quantity of fresh. All other herbs should be used fresh – especially basil, chervil, parsley, chives, tarragon, coriander and dill.

Basil

Basil is closely associated with Provençal cuisine. It has a sweet and heady flavour, which goes with most summer dishes. You can now buy it fresh anywhere or grow it in a container on your windowsill.

Chervil

A little-known herb in the UK, yet it will give a salad or soup its character and the most fragrant aroma. You can easily grow it from seed on your windowsill.

Chives

Chives are part of the onion family. They will add pungency to any salad, soup or savoury dish.

Flat-leaf parsley

Also known as Italian parsley, this has a cleaner flavour than the curly-leaf variety. The leaves are more tender, too, with a vivid colour. It is used widely both raw and cooked.

Clockwise from bottom left: thyme, bay leaves, fresh basil, chives, flat-leaf parsley, rosemary and chervil

Above: bouquet garni

Bouquet garni

This is a bunch of aromatic herbs used to flavour a dish or sauce. The classic bouquet garni is made with sprigs of thyme, a bay leaf and sprigs of parsley. Your favourite herbs – sage, tarragon, marjoram – could also be included.

Lardons

These little pieces of diced bacon are used a great deal in French cuisine, giving a characteristic rusticity to many dishes. The bacon, which can be smoked or unsmoked, is taken from the pork belly, cut into slices about 5–8 mm (1/4–1/3 in) thick, then diced.

You can now buy them ready cut from most supermarkets.

Lettuce

Most varieties of lettuce are now available all year round. My favourite winter varieties are escarole, frisée, lamb's lettuce and chicory (see page 10), while in the summer I favour radicchio, rocket, Webb's, oak leaf and watercress. All sorts of dressings can be prepared impromptu, based on extra-virgin olive oil and balsamic vinegar, wine vinegar or lemon juice. Seeds, herbs and flavourings, such as mustard, can also be added.

To make a quick, light meal, add any cheese or a poached egg to a green salad. Be careful not to overdress the leaves or they will taste too oily and vinegary, and remember always to add the dressing at the last moment.

Morel mushrooms

I used to gather fresh morels in my native Franche-Comté, and in my opinion they are one of the best wild mushrooms. They have an incredible taste; you must try them at home. Fresh morels can be difficult to obtain but the dried variety has much more flavour and retains a good texture.

To use them, simply cover with plenty of warm water and soak for a few hours to rehydrate them. With a slotted spoon, lift out the mushrooms and wash them thoroughly under cold running water to remove any sand from the honeycomb cap. Cut off the base of the stalk. The soaking water has a tremendous flavour and you can add it to your sauce. Pour it through a cloth or a fine sieve first to remove any sand.

Rosemary

This beautiful herb will add a touch of Provence to your cooking. Use it carefully, though, as it is very strong (you can always add more but you cannot take it away).

Tarragon

A favourite of French cuisine. The beautiful leaves can taste very powerful at the height of summer. You can soften the flavour by boiling it for a few seconds and then refreshing it in cold water so it keeps its colour.

Thyme

There are many varieties of thyme but the best known are common thyme, which is used in most rustic French dishes, and lemon thyme, which is often used with fish.

Clockwise from bottom: frisée, lamb's lettuce and Webb's

Above: Dijon mustard (left) and seed mustard (right)

Mustard

Mustard owes its flavour and colour to the crushed mustard seeds and added vinegar. Almost every nation has its own recipe for mustard which it firmly believes is the best. As a Frenchman, I will use only Dijon mustard or seed mustard (such as Pommery). Dijon mustard is pungent, yet slightly milder than the English counterpart. It is always used in French vinaigrette and to accompany a roast.

Oil

Most of the south of France uses olive oil, while in the north groundnut or sunflower oil are more common.

Olive oil

Olive oil has a wonderful flavour and is a monounsaturated fat, which helps protect against heart attacks and strokes. It also contains vitamin E, which is a powerful antioxidant. For cooking, use an ordinary olive oil. Extra-virgin olive oil should be used only for dressings or for adding to a dish at the last moment. Once it is cooked the beautiful and expensive flavour will disappear.

Olive oil should be stored in a cool place away from light to retain all of its quality.

Groundnut and sunflower oil

Both groundnut oil and sunflower oil are unscented and have a neutral taste. They can be used for either dressing or cooking.

Peppercorns

Freshly milled pepper is always the best. I much prefer to use it for cooking, as its flavour is vastly superior to the ready-ground pepper you can buy.

White pepper, contrary to popular belief, is harvested later than black pepper. It is less aromatic and has a milder flavour, making it more suitable for delicate dishes such as fish sauces.

Pulses

Haricot beans are my favourite and I also like coco and flageolet beans. They are at their best in June and July, when you can buy them fresh. If you use dried beans, soak them overnight in cold water and then discard the water. Always ensure you cook

Above: dried morel mushrooms

dried beans thoroughly, otherwise they are indigestible.

Salt

Salt can be a public enemy in the kitchen. While pâtissiers murder their food with too much sugar, the chef often murders food with salt. Salt is a flavour enhancer but use it carefully. I find the best is fleur de sel (flower salt), which is collected from the sea and untreated. Maldon salt is also very good.

How much salt to add to a dish? There is an easy way to decide. For 100 g (4 oz) food or 100 ml (3½ fl oz) liquid, add one pinch (a three-finger pinch) of salt, which is slightly less than 1 g; it is the best measurement I know.

Shallots

Shallots are part of the onion family. They have a sharper taste and less sweetness than the onion.

Above: shallots (left) and sorrel (right)

Sorrel

Sorrel leaves look like elongated spinach. Once cooked, they turn a brownish green. The flavour is slightly tart and acidic, which goes so well with the richness of salmon. Salmon with sorrel has become a great classic of French cuisine.

Sorrel may be difficult to find on super-market shelves but it grows very well in the wild or in a garden.

Tomatoes

We have become used to having tomatoes all year round, often produced by the hydroponic method, which means they are grown in gravel through which water containing the necessary nutrients is pumped. This cuts the growing time by half but most of those specimens are anaemic, tasteless and insipid. Try to buy sea-sonal tomatoes as much as possible.

The big fat Marmande has a wonderful balance of flesh versus juice and sugar versus acidity. The Roma, a type of plum tomato, can also be very good. You can find Romas during the summer months in most supermarkets. Another favourite of mine is the cherry tomato, picked while still on the vine. It is packed with flavour and colour.

Vanilla

Vanilla pods

The best are from Tahiti, followed by Madagascar. In almost every French house, a vanilla pod is kept buried in a jar of sugar to give the best flavour. Vanilla pods are available in the UK but too often they are of very poor quality – mean and shrivelled. A good vanilla pod is dark brown and shiny, with soft, pliable flesh under your fingers. It hides millions of beautiful seeds, which will release their flavours into cream, milk or sauces.

Vanilla extract

If you cannot find a good vanilla pod, buy the very best vanilla extract – check the label to make sure it is made from the real thing. Never buy vanilla essence, or flavouring; it is simply a chemical cocktail.

Vinegar

In French cuisine we mostly use two vinegars – red wine vinegar and white wine vinegar. The red Cabernet Sauvignon vinegar is sweeter and less acidic. You can find it in some supermarkets and delicatessens. Try to find a good-quality vinegar – it's worth paying for the difference.

Wine

There is no need to buy an expensive wine for cooking. Wine is added to a sauce to give structure, length and acidity to the flavour. You should always boil the wine first to remove all the alcohol.

Red wine

Buy a full-bodied red wine with few tannins and a great ruby colour. Don't buy the most expen-sive, but equally don't buy the cheapest. The quality of the sauce will mirror the wine used. Ones made with Cabernet Sauvignon or Merlot grapes are often the best.

White wine

Use a dry white wine, with a good level of acidity.

Top to bottom: Marmande tomato, plum tomatoes and cherry tomatoes on the vine

Top to bottom: mouli-légumes, oven thermometer, small frying pan, hand-held blender, ovenproof frying pan and griddle pan

EQUIPMENT

Bain marie

A bain marie is a container partly filled with barely simmering water, in which dishes of food are placed to allow a gentle distribution of heat.

Baking trays and roasting tins

Try to buy good-quality, heavy-duty baking trays and roasting tins, so they won't warp and buckle in the heat of the oven.

Balloon whisk

A good whisk should be supple and made of stainless steel.

Blender

A blender is invaluable for making smooth purées and soups. Look for one with a powerful motor and a large capacity. I particularly like the KitchenAid five-speed blender.

Casseroles

For long, slow cooking, nothing is better than a good old-fashioned cast-iron casserole with a lid.

Electric mixer

Buy the best model you can afford. I favour the KitchenAid Ultra Power mixer, which can be used to make bread, meringue and parfaits, for whisking ingredients and mincing meat, and even for making pasta.

Food processor

A powerful food processor has become an indispensable piece of kitchen equipment for chopping, mixing, blending etc. My favourite model is the KitchenAid Ultra Power food processor.

Garlic press

You will have to use a lot of garlic in French cooking. A press is still the best and easiest way to crush your garlic.

Grater

Stainless steel box graters can be used to grate, zest and slice finely and coarsely.

Gratin dishes

These are round or oval china or earthenware dishes with shallow sides in which the food can brown well. It's worth having several in different sizes.

Griddle pan

This is extremely useful for grilling without much fat and gives that marvellous charred flavour to meat, fish and vegetables.

Hand-held blender

A hand-held blender can be bought quite cheaply. It makes puréeing soups and sauces very quick and convenient, as you can use it directly in the saucepan.

Japanese mandoline

This is a very efficient and brilliantly precise piece of equipment for slicing, cutting and grating.

Knives

There are a lot of cheap-looking knives with plastic handles, made of poor-quality steel. Don't be tempted – a good set of knives is essential, so always buy the best you can afford. You need a large chopping knife, a long serrated knife, a vegetable knife, a boning knife and a small knife with a blade about 7.5–10 cm (3–4 in) long. They must be kept sharp at all times.

Melon baller

This can also be used for scooping out the cores from halved apples and pears.

Mixing bowls

Buy plenty of these in different sizes.

Mouli-légumes

A good old traditional mouli-légumes, or vegetable mill, is very useful for puréeing vegetables. Most models come with three or more discs, for producing purées of varying coarseness.

Oven thermometer

The temperature of different ovens can vary

Clockwise from top left: terrine dish, casserole dish, gratin dish with ramekin, balloon whisk and ramekin dish

by as much as 10°C (50°F), which can have a marked effect on your cooking. To ensure that your oven is giving a correct reading, it's worth buying an oven thermometer to check the temperature.

All the recipes in this book were cooked in a fan-assisted oven. If you don't have a fan oven, you may need to add 10°C (50°F) to the temperature when cooking them.

Ramekins
These come in various sizes and can be used for making individual soufflés, crème caramel, etc.

Saucepans and frying pans
At Le Manoir's L'Ecole de Cuisine we use the Analon professional range. These modern, hardwearing pans are light, with a tight-fitting glass lid, and have excellent heat conduction properties. They are also non-stick, which is always a good feature to have, as it means you don't need to use so much fat during cooking.

When buying frying pans, look for ones with ovenproof handles, so they can be transferred to the oven to finish cooking the food.

Spatula
A flexible plastic spatula is very handy for scraping out bowls and preventing any waste.

Temperature probe
This is an invaluable piece of equipment for the inexperienced cook. Use it to check the internal temperature of roast meat, pâtés and parfaits, to help you judge when they are done.

Terrine dishes
If you enjoy making pâtés and parfaits, it is a good idea to invest in some lidded terrine dishes in various sizes.

Tongs
Tongs are very useful for turning meat or vegetables when frying.

Conversion tables

Conversions are approximate and have been rounded up or down. Follow one set of measurements only – do not mix metric and Imperial.

Weights		Volume		Measurements	
Metric	**Imperial**	**Metric**	**Imperial**	**Metric**	**Imperial**
15 g	½ oz	25 ml	1 fl oz	0.5 cm	¼ inch
25 g	1 oz	50 ml	2 fl oz	1 cm	½ inch
40 g	1½ oz	85 ml	3 fl oz	2.5 cm	1 inch
50 g	2 oz	150 ml	5 fl oz (¼ pint)	5 cm	2 inches
75 g	3 oz	300 ml	10 fl oz (½ pint)	7.5 cm	3 inches
100 g	4 oz	450 ml	15 fl oz (¾ pint)	10 cm	4 inches
150 g	5 oz	600 ml	1 pint	15 cm	6 inches
175 g	6 oz	700 ml	1¼ pints	18 cm	7 inches
200 g	7 oz	900 ml	1½ pints	20 cm	8 inches
225 g	8 oz	1 litres	1¾ pints	23 cm	9 inches
250 g	9 oz	1.2 litres	2 pints	25 cm	10 inches
275 g	10 oz	1.25 litres	2¼ pints	30 cm	12 inches
350 g	12 oz	1.5 litres	2½ pints		
375 g	13 oz	1.6 litres	2¾ pints		

Oven temperatures		
140°C	275°F	Gas Mk 1
150°C	300°F	Gas Mk 2
160°C	325°F	Gas Mk 3
180°C	350°F	Gas Mk 4
190°C	375°F	Gas Mk 5
200°C	400°F	Gas Mk 6
220°C	425°F	Gas Mk 7
230°C	450°F	Gas Mk 8
240°C	475°F	Gas Mk 9

Weights		Volume	
Metric	**Imperial**	**Metric**	**Imperial**
400 g	14 oz	1.75 litres	3 pints
425 g	15 oz	1.8 litres	3¼ pints
450 g	1 lb	2 litres	3½ pints
550 g	1¼ lb	2.1 litres	3¾ pints
675 g	1½ lb	2.25 litres	4 pints
900 g	2 lb	2.75 litres	5 pints
1.5 kg	3 lb	3.4 litres	6 pints
1.75 kg	4 lb	3.9 litres	7 pints
2.25 kg	5 lb	5 litres	8 pints (1 gal)

STARTERS
and SOUPS

Roquefort, walnut and chicory salad

Roquefort comes from the Auvergne, a region of France that British people have a particular affection for. It is a very rich cheese with a strong, spicy taste. This simple salad is one of the best ways to appreciate its flavour. Make sure the cheese is well chilled before use, so you can crumble it easily. Choose the walnuts and walnut oil carefully; if old, they will taste rancid and unpleasant. Should you wish, you can replace the chicory with any other salad leaves.

serves 4
preparation time: 15 minutes

For the salad:

16 small heads of chicory

1 apple, such as Granny
    Smith or Braeburn

75 g (3 oz) Roquefort cheese

100 g (4 oz) walnuts, chopped

1 celery stick, finely sliced

1 tablespoon finely chopped
    fresh chives

For the dressing:

1 tablespoon Dijon mustard

1 tablespoon white wine
    vinegar

2 tablespoons water

2 tablespoons best-quality
    walnut oil

2 tablespoons extra-virgin
    olive oil

sea salt and freshly ground
    black pepper

1 **Preparing the salad ingredients.** Cut the base off the chicory and remove any damaged outer leaves. Cut each chicory head in half lengthways and set aside.

2 Halve the apple, remove the core and slice or dice finely. Crumble the Roquefort on to a plate and chill while you prepare the dressing.

3 Preparing the dressing. To make the dressing, whisk the mustard, vinegar and water together, then trickle in the walnut oil and olive oil, whisking constantly. Season to taste with 2 pinches of salt and 2 pinches of pepper.

4 Finishing the salad. Mix the dressing with the chicory, walnuts, apple, celery and two-thirds of the Roquefort. Arrange on a large serving dish or individual plates. Scatter the remaining Roquefort over the salad and top with the chopped chives.

Gruyère, ham and mushroom salad with cream and mustard dressing

A simple, everyday salad from my native county, Franche-Comté. Most of my English friends speed past it on their way from Paris to the south of France and in doing so bypass one of the loveliest and most hospitable areas of the country. It produces some of the very best cream and cheeses in France, which are used extensively in its cuisine.

serves 4
preparation time: 20 minutes

For the salad:

300 g (11 oz) smoked ham or *jambon de Paris*

100 g (4 oz) Gruyère cheese

200 g (7 oz) firm, fresh button mushrooms

2 chicory heads

100 g (4 oz) frisée lettuce

100 g (4 oz) lamb's lettuce

1 tablespoon chopped fresh chives

For the dressing:

1 small tablespoon Dijon mustard

5 tablespoons whipping cream

1 tablespoon white wine vinegar

5 tablespoons grapeseed oil or extra-virgin olive oil

sea salt and freshly ground black pepper

1 **Preparing the salad ingredients.** Cut the ham into strips. Slice the cheese and cut that into strips too. Cut the mushrooms into slices 3 mm (1/8 in) thick. Cut the base off the chicory and remove any damaged outer leaves. Cut each chicory head in half lengthways, then slice into 2 cm (3/4 in) chunks.

2 **Making the dressing.** Put the mustard in a small bowl and whisk in the cream, then the white wine vinegar. Gradually whisk in the oil and then season to taste with 2 pinches of sea salt and 2 pinches of black pepper.

3 **Finishing the salad.** Put the chicory, lettuce, ham, cheese and mushrooms in a large bowl or individual bowls, and mix with the dressing. Scatter the chopped chives on top and serve.

Poached asparagus with mayonnaise

One of the truly great spring dishes. Asparagus is now available all year round but home grown is best, and the more local the better. The UK season is very short, lasting from May until June.

This mayonnaise bears no resemblance to commercial products bearing the same name. The taste is full, with an edge of acidity and a delicate piquancy from the cayenne pepper. To help prevent the mayonnaise splitting, ensure that all the ingredients are at room temperature before you start. The reward for this simple creative act is enormous and you will never want to buy bottled mayonnaise again.

serves 4
preparation time: 20 minutes
cooking time: 4–5 minutes

For the mayonnaise:
2 organic or free range egg
   yolks
1 teaspoon Dijon mustard
2 pinches of salt
a pinch of cayenne pepper
300 ml (1/2 pint) groundnut oil
   or any good unscented oil
juice of 1/2 lemon

For the asparagus:
1 kg (21/4 lb) medium-sized
   English asparagus
3 litres (5 pints) water
2 tablespoons salt
sea salt and freshly ground
   black pepper

1 Making the mayonnaise. If you are a masochist like me, use a bowl and balloon whisk; otherwise a hand-held electric beater is fine. Whisk the egg yolks, mustard, salt and cayenne together in the bowl. Gradually, at a slow trickle, whisk in the oil. The mixture will thicken and become a rich straw yellow. This early stage is the most delicate; it is important not to add the oil too fast or the sauce might curdle. (If this happens, put another egg yolk in a clean bowl and slowly whisk in the curdled sauce. When it has all been incorporated, continue with the rest of the oil.)

2 The more oil you add, the thicker the sauce will become. Halfway through, whisk in the lemon juice to thin it down, then continue adding the oil, more speedily now as the mayonnaise should be safe from curdling at this stage. Taste and correct the seasoning. If the mayonnaise is too thick, thin it down with about a tablespoon of warm water. Refrigerate until required.

3 **Preparing the asparagus.** Cut off the woody lower part of the asparagus stems. In a large pan, bring the water to a galloping boil and add the salt.

4 **Cooking the asparagus.** Gently lower the asparagus into the rapidly boiling water, making sure that all the tips are on one side of the pan. Cover with a lid to bring the water back to the boil more quickly. Remove the lid and cook for 4–5 minutes, depending on the thickness of the asparagus; it should be bright green and tender but still a little firm.

5 **Serving the asparagus.** Remove the asparagus with a slotted spoon and drain on a tea towel. You can serve it warm or cold. (If you prefer it cold, plunge it into a bowl of cold water to halt the cooking process and retain the colour and texture.) Arrange the asparagus on a large dish and season lightly with sea salt and black pepper. Serve the mayonnaise separately.

Poached artichokes with mustard vinaigrette

The first artichokes of the season are imported from Provence in April but we have to wait until June or July for the English ones. Try to buy large, fat globes that feel heavy for their size, with healthy-looking leaves and no discoloration.

Children love this dish, as it is so much fun to eat. You have to pull the leaves off one by one, dip them into the mustardy dressing, then scrape off the tender flesh from the base of the leaf with your teeth. When all the leaves have gone, pull out and discard the chalky bits (the choke), so you can eat the heart.

serves 4
preparation time: 15 minutes
cooking time: 25–30 minutes

For the artichokes:
3 litres (5 pints) water
40 g (1½ oz) salt
4 large globe artichokes
4 slices of lemon

For the mustard vinaigrette:
1 tablespoon Dijon mustard
1 tablespoon white wine vinegar
5 tablespoons water
a pinch of salt
a pinch of freshly ground white pepper
120 ml (4 fl oz) groundnut oil (or any good unscented oil)
1 small shallot, finely chopped

1 **Preparing the artichokes.** In a large saucepan, bring the water to the boil with the salt. Meanwhile, break off the stalks from the artichokes by holding the head and twisting off the stalk: it should remove some of the tough fibres with it. Tie a lemon slice to the base of each artichoke with string – this prevents discoloration during cooking.

2 **Cooking the artichokes.** Add the artichokes to the boiling water and bring back to a gentle simmer, with a few bubbles just breaking the surface. Place a plate over the artichokes to keep them submerged and cook for 25–30 minutes, depending on their size; the leaves should peel away easily when they are done. Turn off the heat and leave them to cool in their cooking water.

3 **Making the vinaigrette and serving the artichokes.** While the artichokes are cooking, whisk together all the ingredients for the vinaigrette in a small bowl. Taste and correct the seasoning if required. Serve the barely warm artichokes with the mustard vinaigrette on the side.

Chicken liver parfait

Smooth, silky, melting and completely delicious. This pâté remains one of the most popular dishes in the Le Petit Blanc brasseries. It's a bit rich, but who cares? Accompanied by a glass of red wine and a thick slice of toasted bread, it is the perfect treat to share with friends around your table. You can serve the parfait with pickles, chutney or soused vegetables.

serves 8–10
preparation time: 30 minutes,
   plus 6 hours' soaking
cooking time: 40–50 minutes

For soaking the chicken livers:
200 ml (7 fl oz) milk
200 ml (7 fl oz) water
4 pinches of salt

For the parfait:
400 g (14 oz) fresh chicken livers
100 ml (3¹/₂ fl oz) dry Madeira
100 ml (3¹/₂ fl oz) ruby port

1 large shallot, finely chopped
1 teaspoon finely chopped fresh thyme
50 ml (2 fl oz) cognac
1 garlic clove, crushed
400 g (14 oz) unsalted butter, diced
5 organic or free range eggs
sea salt and freshly ground black pepper

To cover the parfait:
150 g (5 oz) butter, melted

1 **Preparing the chicken livers.** Check the chicken livers carefully and cut off any trace of green. Place the livers in a large bowl, add the milk, water and salt and leave to soak for 6 hours. Drain well and rinse.

2 **Cooking off the alcohol.** On a high heat, in a small saucepan, boil the Madeira, port, shallot and thyme until reduced by half. Add the cognac and garlic and boil for a further 10 seconds. Remove from the heat and leave to cool.

3 **Making the parfait.** Pre-heat the oven to 150°C/300°F/Gas Mark 2. On a low heat, in a small saucepan, melt the diced butter without letting it colour. Remove from the heat and keep warm. In a blender, purée the chicken livers for 30 seconds; add the alcohol and shallot mixture and the eggs; blend for 3–4 minutes, until silky smooth. With the machine running, gradually pour in the warm melted butter. Add 10 pinches of salt and 4 pinches of pepper.

4 **Cooking the parfait.** Strain the mixture through a fine sieve and pour it into a 23 x 9 x 7.5 cm (9 x 3½ x 3 in) terrine mould. Place the terrine in a roasting tin and slide it on to the oven shelf. Cover loosely with a piece of buttered greaseproof paper and pour boiling water into the roasting tin until it reaches two-thirds of the way up the side of the terrine mould. Cook for 40–50 minutes. The top of the parfait will be slightly raised and rounded, with no dip in the centre. The inside should be 65–70°C (150–160°F); if you have a temperature probe, check this.

5 **Finishing the parfait.** Remove the terrine from the oven and leave to cool at room temperature for 2 hours. Then pour the melted butter over the top to prevent discoloration. Cover with cling film and refrigerate for at least a day, preferably 2 days (after 2 days the depth of flavour will improve dramatically). To serve, dip the terrine mould into a roasting tin of hot water, then dip a knife blade in hot water and slide it against the sides of the terrine to loosen the parfait. Turn out on to a serving plate. Dip a knife blade in hot water again and cut thick slices on to the plate.

Pâté de campagne

Surprisingly quick and easy; a great dish to grace every day or a dinner party. Even the *grande dame* of British cuisine, Delia Smith, is embracing this magnificent coarse pâté with great Francophile fervour! Try it for yourself. It is best prepared about two days in advance, so the flavours have time to mature. You could replace the pork with veal. Gherkins or pickled vegetables are the best garnish, not forgetting a hunk of rustic bread.

serves 8
preparation time: 20 minutes
cooking time: 1 hour

- 250 g (9 oz) boned pork shoulder, cut into 3 cm (1¼ in) dice
- 250 g (9 oz) boned belly of pork, cut into 3 cm (1¼ in) dice
- 250 g (9 oz) smoked streaky bacon, cut into 3 cm (1¼ in) dice
- 300 g (11 oz) pig's liver, cut into 3 cm (1¼ in) dice
- 1 medium organic or free range egg
- 6 pinches of salt
- 2 pinches of freshly ground black pepper
- 4 juniper berries, crushed
- 2 pinches of five-spice powder
- ½ teaspoon fresh thyme leaves, finely chopped
- 50 ml (2 fl oz) white wine, boiled for 30–40 seconds to evaporate the alcohol
- 2 tablespoons cognac
- 20 g (¾ oz) pistachios (or almonds or hazelnuts)
- 1 fresh bay leaf
- 2 sprigs of fresh thyme

1 **Chopping the meats.** Pre-heat the oven to 160°C/325°F/Gas Mark 3. In a food processor, using the pulse button, chop the pork shoulder until you have a coarse mince texture. Using a spatula, transfer the meat from the food processor to a large mixing bowl. Proceed in exactly the same way with the belly of pork, the smoked streaky bacon and the liver, combining all the meats in the bowl.

2 **Preparing the pâté.** Add the egg, salt, pepper, juniper berries, five-spice powder, chopped thyme, white wine, cognac and nuts to the bowl and vigorously mix everything together with a large wooden spoon.

3 **Filling the terrine.** Tip the mixture into a 23 x 9 x 7.5 cm (9 x 3½ x 3 in) terrine mould and, with the edge of a spoon, press and pack the meat down into the mould. Tap the terrine a couple of times on the work surface to ensure that there are no air pockets and that the meat is compact. Press the bay leaf and thyme sprigs on to the top of the mixture.

4 **Cooking the pâté.** Cover loosely with a piece of buttered greaseproof paper, then place the terrine in a roasting tin and slide on to the oven shelf. Pour boiling water into the roasting tin until it reaches two-thirds of the way up the side of the terrine mould. Cook for 1 hour. The top of

the pâté should be slightly rounded. The inside should be 65–70°C (150–160°F); if you have a temperature probe, check this. Remove the terrine from the oven, leave to cool at room temperature for 2 hours, then cover with cling film. Refrigerate for 2 days so the flavours mature. To serve, dip a knife blade in hot water and slide it against the sides of the terrine to loosen the pâté. Turn the terrine upside down on a tray and tap the base to free it from its mould. Carve generous slices on to plates.

Maman Blanc's vegetable and chervil soup

A small tribute to 'Maman Blanc', and I should say to Papa Blanc, too, as most of the vegetables would come from his garden. The success of this soup depends upon the freshness and quality of the vegetables used. However, you can vary the vegetables and herbs according to the season. Chervil is one of my favourite herbs and is very popular in France but less well known in the UK, although you can now find it in most supermarkets.

serves 4–6
preparation time: 20 minutes
cooking time: 10–12 minutes

For the soup:

1 onion, cut into 3 mm (1/8 in) dice

1 garlic clove, crushed

2 large carrots, cut into slices 3 mm (1/8 in) thick

3 celery sticks, cut into slices 5 mm (1/4 in) thick

2 leeks, 2 outer layers removed, cut into slices 1 cm (1/2 in) thick

15 g (1/2 oz) unsalted butter

1 large courgette, halved lengthways and cut into slices 5 mm (1/4 in) thick

2 ripe tomatoes, roughly chopped

1 litre (13/4 pints) boiling water

a large handful of fresh chervil, roughly chopped

sea salt and freshly ground white pepper

To finish the soup:

1 tablespoon crème fraîche (or a large tub!) or 15 g (1/2 oz) unsalted butter

1 **Sweating the vegetables.** On a medium heat, in a large saucepan, soften the onion, garlic, carrots, celery and leeks in the butter for 5 minutes, without letting them colour (this helps to extract maximum flavour). Season with 8 pinches of salt and 2 pinches of white pepper.

2 **Cooking the soup.** Add the courgette, tomatoes and boiling water (using boiling water reduces the cooking time and also helps keep the colours bright). Boil fast for 5–7 minutes, until the vegetables are just tender. Stir in the chopped chervil.

3 **Finishing the soup.** Whisk in the crème fraîche or butter (or both, if you wish!). Taste and correct the seasoning if necessary, then serve. This soup can be puréed in a blender if you prefer a smooth texture.

French onion soup

The humble onion is very much part of the French culinary anthology. It was probably also responsible for the second invasion of England by the French. I still remember when I first came to England, seeing Frenchmen riding very drunkenly on bicycles, loaded with magnificent entwined onions.

The quality of the onions is crucial in this recipe. We want both high acidity and high sugar levels to create a fully flavoured soup. The best onions are Pink Roscoff; Spanish onions, although lacking in acidity, will also work. If you like a strong onion flavour, caramelize the onions for a further 15 minutes, until very dark brown.

serves 4
preparation time: 25 minutes
cooking time: 40–50 minutes

For the soup:

50 g (2 oz) unsalted butter, diced

4 medium Roscoff or Spanish onions, cut in half and then sliced 3 mm (1/8 in) thick

1 heaped tablespoon plain flour

200 ml (7 fl oz) dry white wine, boiled for 30 seconds to remove the alcohol

1.5 litres (2 1/2 pints) boiling water

1 teaspoon sugar (optional)

sea salt and freshly ground black pepper

To serve:

12 slices of baguette, cut 1 cm (1/2 in) thick

150 g (5 oz) Gruyère cheese, grated

1 Softening the onions. Preheat the oven to 200°C/400°F/ Gas Mark 6. On a high heat, in a large non-stick saucepan, melt the butter without letting it brown. Add the onions and soften for 5 minutes, stirring frequently. Season with 10 pinches of salt and 2 pinches of pepper.

2 Caramelizing the onions. Continue cooking the onions for 20–30 minutes to achieve an even, rich brown caramel colour. Stir every 2–3 minutes to prevent burning.

3 **Toasting the flour.** Sprinkle the flour on a baking tray and cook in the oven for 8–10 minutes, until it is very lightly coloured. Stir the flour into the caramelized onions and mix thoroughly.

4 **Finishing the soup.** Gradually stir in the white wine and one third of the boiling water. Whisk well and add the remaining water. Bring to the boil, skim off any impurities from the surface and simmer for 15 minutes. Taste and correct the seasoning, adding the sugar if required.

5 **Making the croûtons and serving the soup.** Arrange the baguette slices on a baking tray and sprinkle two thirds of the grated Gruyère over them. Place under a hot grill for 3–4 minutes to melt and slightly brown the cheese. Serve the soup in bowls, with the croûtons on top. Serve the remaining Gruyère separately.

Watercress soup

This soup celebrates the essence of watercress, cooking it with minimal loss of nutrients, so retaining its fresh, peppery flavour. I add ice to the watercress to halt the cooking process, so that not only the flavour but the vivid colour is preserved.

The pepperiness of watercress can vary, so taste it before cooking. If it is quite mild, leave some of the stalks attached to boost the flavour.

serves 4
preparation time: 15 minutes
cooking time: 20 minutes

1/2 onion, finely chopped

1 leek, 2 outer layers removed, sliced

15 g (1/2 oz) unsalted butter

1 medium potato, peeled and finely sliced

800 ml (1 1/3 pints) boiling water

4 large bunches of watercress, stalks removed

1 handful of spinach, stalks removed

750 ml (1 1/4 pints) iced water (500 ml/17 fl oz water plus 250 g/9 oz ice)

sea salt and freshly ground white pepper

crème fraîche, to serve (optional)

1 **Making the soup base.**
Over a low heat, in a large saucepan, soften the onion and leek in half the butter for 5 minutes.

2 Add the sliced potato and boiling water and season with 10 pinches of salt and 2 pinches of white pepper. Boil fast for 10 minutes, until the potato is tender, then leave to cool.

3 **Cooking the watercress.**
Over a low heat, in a medium saucepan, cook the watercress and spinach in the remaining butter for 2–3 minutes, until wilted. Add the iced water to stop the cooking, then combine with the soup base.

4 **Finishing the soup.** Purée in a blender until very smooth, then strain through a sieve into a clean pan. Reheat gently, then taste and correct the seasoning if necessary. Serve in a large soup tureen or individual bowls, with a swirl of crème fraîche, if liked.

FISH, POULTRY
and MEAT

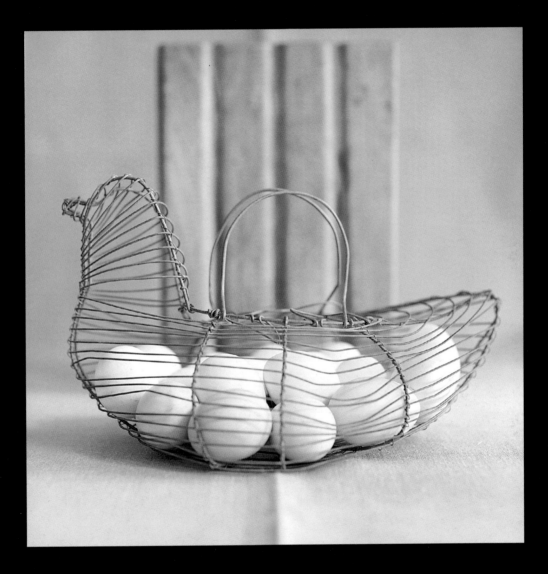

Pan-fried fillet of sea bream with ratatouille and tomato coulis

All the clean, fresh flavours of Provence can be found in this fragrant dish. The obvious time to eat it is in the summer, when the tomatoes are fat and bursting with juices and sweetness and all the vegetables are local and packed with flavour. The ratatouille can be prepared a day in advance and the tomato coulis a few hours in advance.

serves 4
preparation time: 20 minutes
cooking time: 25–35 minutes

For the ratatouille:

2 onions, cut into 2 cm (3/4 in) dice

4 sprigs of fresh thyme

4 tablespoons olive oil

4 garlic cloves, crushed

2 large red peppers, seeded and cut into 2 cm (3/4 in) dice

2 large courgettes, cut in half lengthways and cut into 2 cm (3/4 in) dice

1 medium aubergine, cut in half lengthways and cut into 2 cm (3/4 in) dice

2 tablespoons tomato purée

4 plum tomatoes, chopped

sea salt and freshly ground black pepper

For the tomato coulis:

200 g (7 oz) very ripe cherry tomatoes

2 tablespoons extra-virgin olive oil

2 pinches of sugar (if the tomatoes aren't ripe enough)

sea salt and freshly ground black pepper

For the sea bream:

4 sea bream fillets, descaled

1 tablespoon extra-virgin olive oil, plus extra for drizzling

juice of 1/2 lemon

sea salt and freshly ground black pepper

1 **Making the ratatouille.** Pre-heat the oven to 200°C/ 400°F/Gas Mark 6. On a medium heat, in a large saucepan, soften the onions and thyme in the olive oil for 3–4 minutes, without letting them colour. Add the garlic, red peppers, courgettes, aubergine, 8 pinches of salt and 4 pinches of pepper and cook for 2 minutes longer.

2 Stir in the tomato purée and chopped tomatoes. Cook over a medium heat, with a lid on, for 15–20 minutes, until the vegetables are tender. Taste and correct the seasoning if necessary, then set aside.

3 **Making the tomato coulis.** In a blender, or with a hand-held blender, purée the cherry tomatoes with the extra-virgin olive oil, 2 pinches of salt and a pinch of pepper. Taste and add the sugar if necessary, then strain and set aside.

4 **Frying the sea bream.** Slash each fillet 3 times with a sharp knife (this allows the heat to penetrate more easily). Season with 4 pinches of salt and 2 of pepper. Over a high heat, in a large, oven-proof frying pan, heat the oil. Sear the fillets on the flesh side for 30–40 seconds in the hot olive oil. Turn the fillets over and cook for 2–3 minutes. Transfer to the oven and cook for 2–3 minutes longer, depending on thickness. Taste and correct the seasoning, if necessary, then sprinkle the lemon juice over the fillets.

5 **Finishing the dish.** Reheat the ratatouille and gently warm the tomato coulis, making sure it does not boil (if it did it would become grainy and lose all its freshness). Arrange the ratatouille in the middle of 4 soup plates and top with the sea bream fillets. Spoon the tomato coulis around and then drizzle with the best extra-virgin olive oil.

Roasted monkfish with herb purée and mustard beurre blanc

This dish will grace your table at any dinner party. Monkfish is a great fish and is now available in most supermarkets. Its firm, tasty flesh makes it a favourite and a prized catch.

Beurre blanc is not as daunting as it sounds. Rich in butter, it defies all the rules of nutrition but is delicious to eat and simple to make. It can be prepared half an hour in advance, while the herb purée can be prepared one day in advance.

serves 4
preparation time: 45 minutes
cooking time: 25–30 minutes

For the herb purée:

1 litre (1³/₄ pints) water

100 g (4 oz) flat-leaf parsley leaves, washed and drained

1 large shallot, finely chopped

50 g (2 oz) unsalted butter

200 g (7 oz) watercress leaves, washed and drained

400 g (14 oz) spinach, stalks removed, washed and drained

100 ml (3¹/₂ fl oz) whipping cream

sea salt and freshly ground white pepper

For the beurre blanc:

¹/₂ shallot, finely sliced

2 tablespoons dry white wine

1 tablespoon white wine vinegar

50 ml (2 fl oz) water

120 g (4¹/₂ oz) chilled unsalted butter, diced

1 heaped teaspoon Pommery mustard

¹/₂ teaspoon lemon juice

sea salt and freshly ground white pepper

For the monkfish:

4 x 175 g (6 oz) slices of monkfish, cut from the middle of the fillet

2 tablespoons olive oil

sea salt and freshly ground white pepper

1 **Blanching the parsley.** On a high heat, in a large saucepan, bring the water to the boil and add the parsley leaves. Cook for 4 minutes, until tender, then lift out with a slotted spoon and place in iced water to stop the cooking and retain the colour. Drain and set aside.

2 **Making the herb purée.** On a medium heat, in a large saucepan, soften the shallot in the butter for 5 minutes without colouring. Turn up the heat to high, add the watercress and spinach, cover with a lid and cook for 1 minute, stirring from time to time. Remove the lid and stir for a further minute, until wilted.

3 Add the blanched parsley, cream, 8 pinches of salt and 2 pinches of white pepper. Stir, return to the boil and remove the pan from the heat. Pour the contents of the pan into a food processor and process for 20–30 seconds to make a coarse purée. Taste and correct the seasoning if required.

4 Spread the herb purée on to a large baking tray to allow it to cool down quickly (this prevents loss of colour). Set aside.

5 **Making the beurre blanc.** On a high heat, in a small saucepan, boil the shallot, white wine, white wine vinegar and 1 pinch of white pepper. Let it reduce for 3–4 minutes, until almost all the liquid has evaporated (if it doesn't, the sauce will be too vinegary and strong).

6 Add the water, then gradually whisk in the diced butter to create a smooth sauce. Whisk in the mustard, lemon juice and 1 pinch of salt. If you wish, you can whizz the sauce with a hand-held blender at this stage to make it even smoother. Taste and correct the seasoning if necessary. Keep the beurre blanc warm by putting the pan in a bain marie (a bowl or roasting tin of hot water) while you cook the monkfish.

7 Cooking the monkfish and serving. Pre-heat the oven to 180°C/350°F/Gas Mark 4. Pat the monkfish slices dry and season them with 2 pinches of salt and 2 pinches of white pepper. On a medium heat, in a large frying pan, heat the olive oil and fry the monkfish slices in it for 5–6 minutes on each side. Place in the oven for 3–4 minutes to finish the cooking. To serve, reheat the herb purée and divide between 4 plates. Top with the monkfish fillet and spoon the mustard beurre blanc around.

Pan-fried salmon fillet with sorrel sauce

Sorrel used to grow wild in the fields of my native Franche-Comté and you can find it in the UK, too. It is very acidic and can be overwhelming, but combined with the mellow taste of salmon it works very well. Please try to buy the best salmon you can find. I am very well aware that wild or organic salmon costs a lot more than farmed salmon but it is definitely worth it.

serves 4
preparation time: 20 minutes
cooking time: 10 minutes

For the sorrel sauce:

1 shallot, finely chopped

50 ml (2 fl oz) dry white wine

100 g (4 oz) sorrel, stalks removed

100 ml (3¹/₂ fl oz) whipping cream

juice of ¹/₄ lemon

1 plum tomato, seeded (but not skinned) and cut into 5 mm (¹/₄ in) dice

sea salt and freshly ground white pepper

For the salmon:

4 x 175 g (6 oz) wild or organic salmon fillets, cut across from a medium-sized fish, skinned

20 g (³/₄ oz) unsalted butter

juice of ¹/₂ lemon

sea salt and freshly ground white pepper

1 **Making the sorrel sauce.** On a high heat, in a small pan, boil the shallot and white wine for 30 seconds, to evaporate the alcohol.

2 Add the sorrel, cream, lemon juice, 2 pinches of salt and 2 pinches of white pepper. Bring to the boil and cook, stirring, for 1 minute, until the cream has thickened a little. Do not be alarmed if the sorrel starts changing colour from bright green to a brownish green. This is completely normal. Add the diced tomato and set aside.

3 **Cooking the salmon.** Season the salmon fillets with 2 pinches of salt and 2 pinches of white pepper. On a medium heat, in a large frying pan, melt the butter until it is foaming. Add the salmon fillets and fry for 2–3 minutes on each side, depending on the thickness of the fillet.

4 Remove from the heat and squeeze a little lemon juice over each fillet. Reheat the sorrel sauce and divide it between 4 serving plates. Arrange the salmon on the plates and serve immediately.

Chicken fricassée with vinegar and herbs

A little jewel of family cuisine. The success of this dish depends very much on the quality of the ingredients. Try to choose an organic or free range chicken and also a good red wine vinegar, such as a Cabernet Sauvignon. The dish can be prepared one day in advance and then reheated in the oven at 150°C/300°F/Gas Mark 2. A generous helping of French beans makes an excellent accompaniment.

serves 4
preparation time: 30 minutes
cooking time: 40 minutes

For the chicken fricassée:

4 organic or free range chicken drumsticks and 4 thighs

1 tablespoon olive oil

5 tablespoons good-quality red wine vinegar

15 g (1/2 oz) unsalted butter

100 ml (3 1/2 fl oz) dry white wine

4 garlic cloves, peeled but left whole

1 ripe medium tomato, finely chopped

2 sprigs of fresh tarragon, chopped

1 tablespoon fresh flat-leaf parsley, roughly chopped

sea salt and freshly ground black pepper

For the sautéed potatoes:

4 medium potatoes, such as Desiree, Maris Piper or King Edward, peeled (if organic, leave the skin on) and cut into 2 cm (3/4 in) dice

2 tablespoons olive oil

10 g (1/4 oz) unsalted butter

1 small handful of fresh flat-leaf parsley, roughly chopped

1/2 shallot, finely chopped

sea salt and freshly ground black pepper

1 **Browning the chicken.** Preheat the oven to 150°C/300°F/ Gas Mark 2. On a high heat, in a large casserole, fry the chicken pieces in the olive oil for 5 minutes, until golden brown. Season with 4 pinches of salt and 2 pinches of pepper.

2 **Glazing the chicken.** Spoon out the fat from the casserole. Add the vinegar and butter and boil for 10 seconds, until the vinegar has reduced. Stir to coat the chicken pieces in the reduced vinegar and butter.

3 **Baking the chicken.** Add the white wine, bring to the boil for a few seconds, then add the garlic, tomato and tarragon. Cover the casserole, transfer to the oven and cook for 30 minutes (the liquid should not boil but should cook at a very low simmer, with just one or two bubbles barely breaking the surface). The chicken will be juicy and tender.

4 **Sautéing the potatoes.** On a high heat, in a large frying pan, fry the diced potatoes in the olive oil for 12–15 minutes, stirring frequently, until golden brown and tender. Season with 4 pinches of sea salt and 2 pinches of pepper. Reduce the heat and add the butter, being careful not to let it burn. Finally stir in the parsley and shallot. Taste and adjust the seasoning if necessary.

5 **Finishing the chicken and serving.** Remove the chicken from the oven. Taste and correct the seasoning if required. Skim any fat from the surface. Arrange the chicken pieces and sautéed potatoes on a large platter or 4 serving plates and sprinkle with the parsley. Serve the cooking juices separately.

Grilled marinated chicken breast with courgette ribbons

I do urge you to try this dish. Although it looks quite long it is very simple. It can be prepared a day in advance and then takes only a few minutes to cook. You could experiment with other herbs in the marinade, or even spices if you wish.

serves 4
preparation time: 25 minutes,
  plus at least 6 hours' marinating
cooking time: 6 minutes

For the grilled chicken:

4 boneless, skinless organic or free range chicken breasts

6 tablespoons extra-virgin olive oil

juice of 1/2 lemon

2 garlic cloves, crushed

1/2 teaspoon finely chopped fresh thyme

1/2 teaspoon finely chopped fresh rosemary

sea salt and coarsely ground black pepper

For the marinated courgettes:

4 large but firm courgettes, cut lengthways into slices 3 mm (1/8 in) thick

1/2 garlic clove, crushed

8 fresh basil leaves, torn

4 tablespoons extra-virgin olive oil

sea salt and freshly ground black pepper

For the tomato dressing:

4 tomatoes, seeded (but not skinned) and cut into 5 mm (1/4 in) dice

1 shallot, finely chopped

8 tablespoons extra-virgin olive oil

4 tablespoons water

1 teaspoon white wine vinegar

1–2 pinches of sugar (optional)

sea salt

1 **Preparing the chicken breasts.** Slice each chicken breast horizontally in half, leaving it joined at one side, so you can open it up like a book. Place between 2 sheets of clingfilm and flatten with a meat mallet or rolling pin (be careful not to do this too forcefully or the texture of the meat will be ruined and it will taste dry).

2 **Marinating the chicken. Mix** the olive oil, lemon juice, crushed garlic, thyme, rosemary and 4 pinches of black pepper together to make a marinade. Put the chicken breasts in a large shallow dish, cover them with the marinade, then cover the dish with cling film and leave to marinate in the refrigerator for at least 6 hours.

3 **Marinating the courgettes.** Mix the courgette slices with the garlic, basil, olive oil, 6 pinches of salt and 4 pinches of pepper. Cover and leave to marinate in the fridge for at least 6 hours.

4 **Making the tomato dressing.** Whisk the tomatoes, shallot, oil, water and vinegar together with 4 pinches of salt. Taste and correct the seasoning, adding the sugar if necessary. Set aside in a small saucepan.

5 **Grilling the chicken.** Season the chicken breasts with 4 pinches of salt. On a very hot ridged griddle pan, cook 2 chicken breasts for 2 minutes on each side, then remove and set aside. Repeat with the remaining chicken breasts.

6 **Finishing the dish.** Transfer the courgettes and their juices to a large saucepan. Cover and cook over a high heat for 2 minutes, until just tender. Meanwhile, gently heat the tomato dressing; don't let it boil or the flavour will be spoiled. Remove the courgettes from the pan with a slotted spoon. Put them on 4 plates with the chicken, spoon over the dressing and serve.

Coq au vin

This dish demonstrates what is truly great about French cuisine – the conviviality, the friends and laughter, the simple, hearty food, the rustic bread dipped into the sauce, and the heady red wine that will be drunk. Time stops. That is why this dish has become almost timeless and loved by nearly everyone. Despite a certain degree of complication it is a must for a fantastic dinner party.

serves 4

preparation time: 1 hour,
   plus 24 hours' marinating

cooking time: 1 hour

1.5 kg (3¼ lb) organic or free range chicken, cut into 10 pieces (you could ask your butcher to do this)

1 heaped tablespoon plain flour

2 tablespoons olive oil

sea salt and freshly ground black pepper

For the marinade:

1 litre (1¾ pints) full-bodied red wine, such as Shiraz or Cabernet Sauvignon

3 medium carrots, cut into slanted slices 1 cm (½ in) thick

2 celery sticks, cut into slices 1 cm (½ in) thick

20 baby onions, peeled but left whole

1 teaspoon black peppercorns, crushed

1 bouquet garni (a few parsley stalks, 2 bay leaves and 6 sprigs of thyme, tied together)

For the garnish:

1 tablespoon olive oil

200 g (7 oz) smoked streaky bacon, rind removed, diced

400 g (14 oz) small button mushrooms, trimmed

1 tablespoon chopped fresh flat-leaf parsley

1 **Marinating the chicken.** Bring the red wine to the boil and boil until reduced by a third, to remove the alcohol and concentrate the colour and flavour. Leave to cool. In a bowl, mix the chicken pieces, carrots, celery, baby onions, peppercorns and bouquet garni together and pour the cooled red wine over them. Cover with cling film, refrigerate and leave to marinate for 24 hours.

2 Place a colander over a large bowl and put the chicken mixture in it to drain off the marinade. Leave for a minimum of 1 hour to remove excess liquid. Separate the chicken, vegetables and herbs, and pat dry with kitchen paper. Season the chicken with 4 pinches of salt and 4 pinches of freshly ground black pepper. Reserve the liquid.

3 **Toasting the flour.** Pre-heat the oven to 200°C/400°F/Gas Mark 6. Sprinkle the flour on a baking tray and cook in the oven for 8–10 minutes, until it is very lightly coloured. Set aside. Reduce the oven temperature to 150°C/300°F/Gas Mark 2.

4 **Frying the chicken.** On a high heat, in a large, heavy-based casserole, heat the olive oil and colour the chicken pieces in it for 5–7 minutes on each side. With a slotted spoon, transfer the chicken to a plate and set aside. Add the drained vegetables and herbs to the casserole. Lower the heat to medium high and cook for 5 minutes, until lightly coloured.

5 **Making the sauce.** Spoon out most of the fat from the casserole, add the toasted flour and stir into the vegetables for a few seconds. On a medium heat, whisk in the wine marinade little by little; this will create a sauce and prevent lumps forming. Bring to the boil and skim any impurities from the surface. The wine marinade will be slightly thickened and have the consistency of a light sauce. Add the chicken pieces and return to the boil. Cover with a lid and cook in the pre-heated oven for 30 minutes.

6 **Finishing the sauce.** If you wish you can serve the coq au vin as it is. But should you prefer a richer, more powerful sauce, drain it through a colander and, on a high heat, boil the sauce until it has reduced by one third. It should have acquired more body and become a rich, vinous colour. Pour the sauce back over the chicken and vegetables.

7 **Cooking the garnish.** Over a medium heat, in a medium non-stick frying pan, heat the olive oil and cook the diced bacon in it for 30 seconds. Add the button mushrooms and cook for a further 4 minutes. Season to taste with salt and pepper. Mix the diced bacon and button mushrooms into the coq au vin. Sprinkle with the parsley and serve piping hot, straight from the casserole.

Chicken with morel and sherry sauce

This is a dish that you must cook for your friends. It is a classic of French cuisine and comes from my own region, Franche-Comté. It is not particularly light, but who cares when it is so good! Two advantages are that it is quick and easy to make and it can be prepared an hour in advance. I have replaced the usual Jura wine with dry sherry, which works very well. A dry Jura white wine would be perfect to accompany this dish.

serves 4
preparation time: 30 minutes
  plus 1 hour's soaking
cooking time: 35 minutes

For the morel and sherry
   sauce:

25 g (1 oz) dried morel
   mushrooms

250 g (9 oz) very firm button
   mushrooms, cut into
   quarters

120 ml (4 fl oz) dry sherry,
   boiled for 30 seconds to
   evaporate the alcohol

400 ml (14 fl oz) double cream

a pinch of salt

For the chicken:

4 boneless, skinless organic
   or free range chicken
   breasts, weighing about
   175 g (6 oz) each

15 g (1/2 oz) butter

sea salt and freshly ground
   black pepper

For the leeks:

1 litre (13/4 pints) water

10 g (1/4 oz) salt

10 g (1/4 oz) butter

2 leeks (top green part
   discarded), 2 outer layers
   removed, cut into 2 cm
   (3/4 in) chunks

1 **Soaking the mushrooms.**
Soak the morels for at least
1 hour in 250 ml (8 fl oz)
tepid water. Drain, reserving
the soaking liquid, and wash
the morels in plenty of cold
running water to remove as
much sand as possible from
the little holes. Drain again,
squeezing out excess water,
and set aside. Strain the
reserved soaking liquid
through a very fine sieve or
a piece of muslin to get rid
of any sand and set that
aside too.

2 **Frying the chicken.** Season
the chicken breasts with 4
pinches of salt and 2 pinches
of pepper. On a medium heat,
in a large frying pan, heat the
butter until it is foaming. Add
the chicken breasts and
colour lightly for about 3 minutes on each side. Remove
from the pan and set aside.

3 **Making the sauce.** On a medium heat, in the pan in which the chicken was fried, soften the morels and button mushrooms in the remaining fat for 1–2 minutes. Season with a pinch of salt, then add the boiled sherry, 100 ml (3¹/₂ fl oz) of the reserved morel soaking liquid and the double cream. Bring to the boil and place the chicken back in the pan; the cream sauce must cover it. Lower the heat to the gentlest possible simmer (with just one bubble breaking the surface) and cook for 13–15 minutes, depending on the size of the chicken breasts.

4 **Cooking the leeks.** Over a high heat, in a large saucepan, bring the water, salt and butter to the boil. Add the leeks, cover with a lid and cook on full boil for 5–10 minutes, until tender. Drain well and keep warm.

5 **Finishing the sauce.** When the chicken is done, remove from the pan and keep warm. On full heat, boil the sauce for 6–8 minutes, until it has thickened enough to coat the back of a spoon. Reduce the heat and return the chicken to the sauce to reheat for 2 minutes. Taste and correct the seasoning if required. Arrange the chicken and leeks on 4 serving plates and spoon the sauce over.

Duck breast with sweet potatoes and cherry sauce

A great classic. The sweet acidity of the cherries complements the mellowness of the duck meat. You could use plums instead of cherries. This dish is extremely easy and will dispel the myth that duck is fatty. You will be left with succulent meat, pink all the way through and topped with a crispy skin.

serves 4
preparation time: 40 minutes
cooking time: 30 minutes

For the cherry sauce:

50 ml (2 fl oz) red wine

50 ml (2 fl oz) ruby port

300 g (11 oz) fresh cherries, stoned

1 pinch of five-spice powder

2 pinches of freshly ground cinnamon (or best-quality ready-ground cinnamon)

sea salt and freshly ground black pepper

For the duck:

4 organic or free range duck breasts, about 225 g (8 oz) each, off the bone

sea salt and freshly ground black pepper

For the sweet potato:

1 large sweet potato, about 450 g (1 lb), peeled and cut lengthways into slices 8 mm (1/3 in) thick (you will need only the 4 largest slices)

2 teaspoons groundnut oil (or other good unscented oil)

10 g (1/4 oz) unsalted butter

sea salt and freshly ground black pepper

1 **Making the cherry sauce.** Pre-heat the oven to 180°C/ 350°F/Gas Mark 4. On a high heat, in a medium saucepan, boil the red wine and port until reduced by half. Add the cherries, five-spice powder, cinnamon, a pinch of salt and a pinch of black pepper. Return to the boil and simmer for 2–3 minutes, then remove 20 cherries and set aside.

2 Pour the remaining cherries and sauce into a blender and blend for 2 minutes. Strain through a fine sieve into a small saucepan. Add the reserved cherries to the sauce, then taste and adjust the seasoning if required.

3 **Preparing the duck breasts.**
With a very sharp knife, score the skin of each duck breast 6 or 7 times; be careful not to cut the flesh. Season the duck breasts with 2 pinches of salt and 2 pinches of pepper.

4 **Rendering the fat and cooking the duck breasts.** On a medium-low heat, in a large ovenproof frying pan, cook the duck breasts skin-side down for 10 minutes to melt the fat away and crisp the skin; spoon out excess fat 2 or 3 times. Turn the duck on to its flesh side and sear for 1 minute to seal the juices inside. Turn the duck breasts skin-side down again and place in the hot oven for 4 minutes. Remove from the oven and allow to rest for 4 minutes.

5 **Cooking the sweet potato and serving.** While the skin of the duck is rendering, on a medium heat, in a large ovenproof frying pan, fry the sweet potato slices in the groundnut oil and butter. Colour them for 5–6 minutes on each side, seasoning with 2 pinches of salt and 2 pinches of pepper, then transfer the pan to the oven for 4 minutes to finish the cooking. Serve each duck breast on a slice of roasted sweet potato, with the hot cherries and cherry sauce spooned around.

Pot-au-feu of braised pork belly

Pot-au-feu is a French peasant dish where the meat, vegetables and broth are all cooked together in one pot. It is often made with a plump and tasty chicken rather than pork. In 1664 King Henri IV of France, a good and great PR man, decreed that every peasant should have a *poule au pot*, or 'chicken in a pot', on Sundays. I suppose if the kings that followed him had shared his wisdom and empathy, France might still have a monarchy today…

serves 4
preparation time: 30 minutes
cooking time: 3 hours

1.5 kg (3¼ lb) organic or free range belly of pork, boned and skin removed (leaving a small layer of fat)

3 fresh sage leaves

3 litres (5 pints) water

4 carrots, peeled

6 garlic cloves, peeled but left whole

1 bouquet garni (made with 2 bay leaves, 6 thyme sprigs, 2 sage leaves, 1 rosemary sprig and 1 marjoram sprig, tied together)

2 celery sticks, cut into 7.5 cm (3 in) lengths and tied together in a bundle

4 banana shallots or ordinary shallots, peeled but left whole

2 leeks, 2 outer layers removed, cut into 7.5 cm (3 in) lengths and tied together in a bundle

½ Savoy cabbage, cut in 4, with the core left in to hold the leaves together

4 medium potatoes, such as Desiree, peeled and cut into quarters

a handful of fresh flat-leaf parsley, roughly chopped

sea salt and freshly ground black pepper

1 **Preparing the pork.** Place the belly of pork fat-side down and season the flesh with 3 pinches of salt and a pinch of pepper. Lay the sage leaves in a line along the centre, then take the thickest part of the belly and roll it up as tightly as possible. Tie a piece of string tightly around the rolled belly; repeat this 5 or 6 times so the meat holds its shape during cooking. In order to hold the belly tightly and tie it at the same time, it is easier to have a friend helping you.

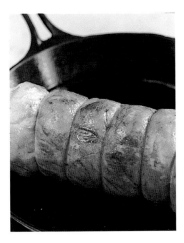

2 Browning the pork. On a medium heat, in a large non-stick frying pan, without oil or butter, fry the rolled pork belly for 12–15 minutes, until golden brown all over.

3 Braising the pork. Place the pork belly in a large casserole. Pour in the water, add 1 tablespoon of salt and bring to the boil over a high heat. With a ladle, skim off any impurities that rise to the surface. Lower the heat and cook on a gentle simmer (with bubbles just breaking the surface) for 1 hour. Fast cooking would make the meat very tough.

4 Cooking the vegetables. Add the carrots, garlic and bouquet garni and cook for a further 30 minutes. Then add all the remaining ingredients except the parsley and cook for 1 hour longer, until the meat and vegetables are tender. Stir in the parsley, adjust the seasoning and serve directly from the pot to the table. Carve the pork in front of your guests or, if you are shy, in the privacy of your kitchen.

Provençal rack of lamb with crushed peas

A marvellous dish that will not take too much of your time. French-trimmed best end of lamb has had the rib bones cleaned and the chine bone cut so you can carve it easily. It is now available in most supermarkets, or your butcher should be able to prepare it for you.

<table>
<tr><td>serves 4</td></tr>
<tr><td>preparation time: 30 minutes</td></tr>
<tr><td>cooking time: 30 minutes</td></tr>
</table>

For the crushed peas:

600 g (1 lb 5 oz) fresh peas, or thawed frozen peas

85 ml (3 fl oz) extra-virgin olive oil

2 tablespoons finely chopped fresh marjoram

2 tablespoons finely chopped fresh mint

juice of 1/2 lemon

sea salt and freshly ground white pepper

For the Provençal breadcrumbs:

75 g (3 oz) thickly cut stale white bread

2 handfuls of fresh flat-leaf parsley, very finely chopped

1 teaspoon very finely chopped fresh thyme

1 teaspoon very finely chopped fresh rosemary

4 tablespoons extra-virgin olive oil

sea salt and freshly ground black pepper

For the lamb:

2 x 350 g (12 oz) racks of lamb, preferably organic, French trimmed

2 tablespoons olive oil

20 g (3/4 oz) unsalted butter

1 tablespoon Dijon mustard

sea salt and freshly ground black pepper

1 **Preparing the peas.** Crush the peas in a food processor, using the pulse button. Do not purée them; you need to retain a lot of texture. Transfer the peas to a medium saucepan and stir in the olive oil, chopped herbs, 6 pinches of salt and a pinch of white pepper. Set aside (you will be cooking the peas and adding the lemon juice just before serving).

2 **Preparing the breadcrumbs.** Crumble the stale bread into the clean food processor and use the pulse button again to process it to crumbs, ensuring that they have a coarse texture and are not powdery (if they are too fine, you will lose the texture). Transfer to a bowl and add the parsley, thyme and rosemary. Stir in the olive oil and season with 2 pinches of salt and a pinch of black pepper.

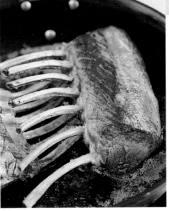

3 **Cooking the lamb.** Pre-heat the oven to 190°C/375°F/Gas Mark 5. Season the racks of lamb with 2 pinches of salt and 2 pinches of black pepper. On a medium heat, in a large ovenproof frying pan, heat the olive oil and butter. Add the lamb and colour the meat of the fillet for 3–4 minutes. Turn it on to its back (fat side) and colour for 3–4 minutes, until golden brown. Transfer the lamb to the oven and roast for 10 minutes.

4 **Finishing the lamb.** Remove the lamb from the oven and brush the mustard all over it, avoiding the bones. Press the racks in the Provençal bread-crumbs, so that every part is coated (this can be done 1–2 hours in advance). Return the lamb to the oven and cook for 8 minutes for medium rare. Turn off the oven, leave the door ajar and allow the lamb to rest for 5 minutes so the meat relaxes and becomes tender.

5 **Finishing the peas.** While the lamb is resting, cook the crushed peas on a medium heat, with a lid on, for 4 minutes. Stir in the lemon juice, then taste and correct the seasoning if necessary. Carve the racks of lamb and serve with the hot crushed peas.

Braised lamb neck fillet with butterbeans and garlic sausage

An excellent rustic dish from the southwest of France, home of the famous cassoulet. The best time to make it is in June or July, when fresh beans are available. If you do use fresh beans, reduce the cooking time by half (that means adding the beans half an hour after the bacon and garlic sausage). It is also excellent in August and September, when the lamb becomes mutton.

This dish can be prepared one day in advance. As an alternative, flageolet or coco beans, if you can find them, can replace the butterbeans.

serves 4

preparation time: 30 minutes,
  plus soaking overnight

cooking time: 2 hours 10 minutes

4 x 300 g (11 oz) lamb or mutton neck fillets, preferably organic, sinews trimmed

25 g (1 oz) unsalted butter

1 tablespoon olive oil

5 ripe tomatoes, cut in quarters and then in half

6 garlic cloves, peeled but left whole

1 bouquet garni (6 sprigs of parsley, 2 bay leaves, 6 sprigs of thyme, 1 sprig of rosemary, tied together)

750 ml (1¼ pints) water

250 g (9 oz) best-quality dried butterbeans, soaked overnight in cold water and then drained

100 g (4 oz) piece of smoked streaky bacon, rind removed, cut into 4

200 g (7 oz) garlic sausage, skinned and roughly chopped

sea salt and freshly ground black pepper

chopped fresh parsley, to garnish

1 **Browning the lamb fillets.** Season the lamb with 2 pinches of salt and 2 pinches of black pepper. On a medium heat, in a large frying pan, heat the butter and olive oil until the butter begins to foam. Sear the lamb fillets for 8 minutes, turning every 2 minutes to achieve a deep golden brown colour. Transfer to a large casserole.

2 **Deglazing the pan.** Spoon the fat from the pan and add 100 ml (3½ fl oz) water to it. Deglaze the pan by scraping the base with a wooden spoon to dissolve the caramelized juices. Pour these juices over the lamb fillets.

3 **Cooking the lamb.** Pre-heat the oven to 110°C/225°F/Gas Mark ¼. Add the tomatoes, garlic, bouquet garni and water to the casserole. Season with 4 pinches of salt and 1 pinch of pepper. Bring to simmering point on the stove, then cover and cook in the pre-heated oven for 1 hour.

4 **Cooking the beans.** After 1 hour, add the drained butterbeans, bacon and chopped garlic sausage to the casserole. Cook for a further hour, then taste and correct the seasoning. Garnish with a little chopped parsley. Serve directly from the oven to the table.

Steak 'Maman Blanc'

For me, this is the best steak in the world, cooked the way my mother used to do it. These great women cooks understood an important basic technique: pan-frying meat in such a way that you can then create the most delectable juices with a simple medium – water. The beef can be replaced with other meat, such as veal, pork or lamb, and as long as you follow the same technique it will work just as well; however, the cooking time will be slightly longer. The best accompaniments are sautéed potatoes (see pages 54–5) and French beans.

serves 4
preparation time: 5 minutes
cooking time: 8–10 minutes

4 x 225 g (8 oz) rump or sirloin steaks, preferably organic, 2 cm (3/4 in) thick, fat trimmed

2 pinches of salt

1 tablespoon coarsely ground black pepper

2 tablespoons olive oil

65 g (2 1/2 oz) unsalted butter

200 ml (7 fl oz) water

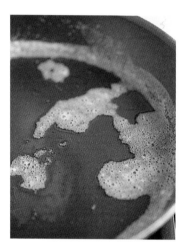

1 **Preparing the steaks.** Season the steaks with the salt and scatter the black pepper over them, pressing it firmly into the steaks on each side.

2 **Heating the pan.** On a medium heat, in a large frying pan, heat the oil and butter until the butter is foaming; it should turn light brown and smell very nutty. It is important to let it reach this stage, so that it will slowly caramelize the surface of the meat. The juices will then create deposits on the pan, which will form the base for the most marvellous pan juices. But don't let the butter burn or it will become carcinogenic, indigestible and develop an unpleasant taste.

3 **Frying the steaks.** Raise the heat to medium high, lay the steaks in the foaming butter and cook for 1 1/2–2 minutes on each side for rare, 3 minutes for medium rare, or 4 minutes for medium. To test if it is done, press the meat gently with your forefinger. For rare, it should be soft and your finger will almost leave an imprint; medium rare will be far more resistant and your finger will not leave an imprint; medium will feel quite firm, because the fibres will be cooked.

4 **Making the sauce.** Transfer the steaks to a warm plate with tongs. Pour the water into the hot pan; there will be a lot of sizzling and the water and butter will create an emulsion. Scrape the base of the pan with a wooden spoon to release the caramelized residue, which will give taste and colour to this succulent juice. Pour the juice on to the steaks and serve immediately.

Calf's liver with persillade

Besides being very nutritious, this dish is extremely popular. There are two main keys to success: firstly, the calf's liver must be very fresh, indicated by a pale pink colour and a firm texture, with no stickiness or smell. Secondly, it must be sliced very thinly, otherwise the texture will be completely wrong. A short cooking time is also essential. The best accompaniment for this dish is Potato Purée (see page 94).

A persillade is a mixture of shallots, garlic and parsley (and sometimes tarragon), frequently used in French cooking. It is usually added to a dish towards the end.

serves 4
preparation time: 10 minutes
cooking time: 5 minutes

For the liver:

4 x 120 g (4^1/$_2$ oz) slices
   of calf's liver, 7–10 mm
   (^{1}/$_3$–^{1}/$_2$ in) thick

40 g (1^1/$_2$ oz) unsalted butter

sea salt and freshly ground
   black pepper

For the persillade:

1 handful of fresh flat-leaf
   parsley

^{1}/$_2$ medium shallot

1 garlic clove

To finish the dish:

100 ml (3^1/$_2$ fl oz) water

juice of ^{1}/$_4$ lemon

1 **Preparing the liver.** Pat the calf's liver dry on kitchen paper, then season the slices evenly on both sides with 4 pinches of salt and 2 pinches of pepper.

2 **Preparing the persillade.** Finely chop the parsley, shallot and garlic, and mix them together. Set aside.

3 **Cooking the liver.** On a medium heat, in a large frying pan, melt the butter until foaming. Add the liver slices and cook for 1½ minutes, until golden brown underneath. Increase the heat and turn the slices of liver over. Cook for a further 1½ minutes.

4 **Finishing the dish.** With a pair of tongs, transfer the liver slices to a serving dish. Quickly add the persillade to the pan. Then add the water and lemon juice and simmer for 10 seconds. Pour the pan juices and persillade over the calf's liver and serve immediately, with Potato Purée, if liked (see page 94).

VEGETABLE
DISHES

Baked pancakes with spinach, mushrooms and Gruyère

A great, warming dish for all seasons. After five years, it remains the bestseller at the Le Petit Blanc brasseries, where it pleases kids and grown-ups alike. It is a dish from my region, Franche-Comté, rich in cream and melting cheese. For meat lovers, you can roll up a fine slice of ham in each pancake. The stuffed pancakes can be prepared one day in advance, ready for baking, and they will be just as good.

serves 4
preparation time: 50 minutes
cooking time: 35 minutes

For the pancakes:

50 g (2 oz) unsalted butter

2 organic or free range eggs

200 ml (7 fl oz) full-fat milk

100 g (4 oz) plain flour

1 tablespoon chopped fresh chives

1 tablespoon chopped fresh flat-leaf parsley

1 tablespoon unscented oil, such as groundnut, for cooking the pancakes

sea salt and freshly ground black pepper

For the filling:

40 g (1½ oz) unsalted butter

300 g (11 oz) spinach, washed, stalks removed, and dried

200 g (7 oz) button mushrooms, fresh and tight, sliced 3 mm (⅛ in) thick

50 g (2 oz) Gruyère cheese, finely grated

sea salt and freshly ground white pepper

For the cream and cheese sauce:

400 ml (14 fl oz) whipping cream

freshly grated nutmeg

50 g (2 oz) Gruyère cheese

sea salt and freshly ground white pepper

1 **Making the pancake batter.** Heat the butter in a small pan until foaming and hazelnut brown. Allow to cool for 2 minutes.

2 In a blender or food processor, liquidize the eggs, milk, flour, 4 pinches of salt and a pinch of black pepper for 1 minute, until smooth. Pour in the butter and liquidize for a further 30 seconds to incorporate it (the butter will give flavour and help prevent the pancakes sticking). Add the chopped chives and parsley, transfer to a bowl, cover with cling film and set aside.

3 **Cooking the spinach.** On a high heat, in a medium frying pan, melt half the butter and throw in the spinach. Cook down the spinach at full heat, stirring all the time, for 2 minutes. Season with a pinch each of salt and white pepper. With the back of the spoon, squeeze the water out of the spinach. Set the spinach aside.

4 **Cooking the mushrooms and finishing the filling.** On a high heat, in a medium frying pan, melt the remaining butter and cook the mushrooms in it for 2 minutes. Season with a pinch each of salt and white pepper. Mix the mushrooms with the spinach, stir in the finely grated Gruyère and set aside.

5 **Cooking the pancakes.** Preheat the oven to 200°C/400°F/ Gas Mark 6. Have ready a baking tray to place the pancakes on once cooked. Heat a small frying pan or, better still, a pancake pan on a medium heat. Add a teaspoon of the oil and swirl it around. The oil must be hot enough to sear and cook the pancakes. Too hot and they will burn; not hot enough and they will be beige and cardboard-like. Practice makes perfect! Ladle just enough pancake batter into the hot pan to cover the surface when swirled. Cook for 15–20 seconds until browned underneath.

6 Slide the spatula underneath and flip the pancake over. Cook for a further 15–20 seconds, then transfer to the baking tray. Repeat, adding more oil as necessary, until all the batter has been used. Try to make the pancakes as thin as possible. You will need 8 all together but you will probably end up with a few extra; either throw these away, if they are practice ones, or wrap them tightly and store in the freezer.

7 **Filling the pancakes.** Spoon the filling along each pancake and roll up tightly (this can be done one day in advance). Arrange all the rolled pancakes in a gratin dish, roughly 25–30 cm (10–12 in) long.

8 **Making the sauce and finishing the dish.** Bring the whipping cream to a rolling boil and add 8 gratings of nutmeg, 2 pinches of salt and a pinch of white pepper. Pour the cream over the pancakes and grate the Gruyère cheese finely over the top. Bake for 20 minutes. The cheese will 'gratinate', creating a golden-brown crust. Serve the bubbling dish from oven to table.

Semolina and Gruyère quenelles with tomato sauce

First I should explain what a quenelle is. It is usually a fish or meat mousse enriched with cream and eggs, shaped into ovals with spoons and then poached. Here we use semolina and Gruyère cheese as a base and shape it more simply by rolling it on a floured surface. It is another dish from my super Mum.

serves 4
preparation time: 30 minutes, plus at least 2 hours' chilling
cooking time: 45 minutes

For the semolina and Gruyère quenelles:

300 ml (1/2 pint) milk

50 g (2 oz) unsalted butter, diced

100 g (4 oz) semolina

50 g (2 oz) plain flour

1 organic or free range egg

1 organic or free range egg yolk

120 g (41/2 oz) Gruyère cheese, finely grated

8 gratings of nutmeg

2 litres (31/2 pints) water

sea salt and freshly ground black pepper

For the tomato sauce:

1 medium onion, finely chopped

2 garlic cloves, crushed

2 sprigs of fresh thyme

3 tablespoons olive oil

4 ripe tomatoes, seeded and chopped

100 g (4 oz) tomato purée

400 ml (14 fl oz) water

3 pinches of sugar (optional)

sea salt and freshly ground black pepper

For the topping:

50 g (2 oz) Gruyère cheese, finely grated on to a tray, so it doesn't stick together

1 **Making the quenelle mixture.** In a medium saucepan, bring the milk to simmering point, then add the butter, semolina and flour all together. Stir with a wooden spoon for 2–3 minutes, until the mixture thickens; remove from the heat and stir in the egg, egg yolk and Gruyère. Season with the nutmeg, 3 pinches of salt and 2 pinches of pepper.

2 With a palette knife, spread the mixture over a baking tray. Leave to cool for 10 minutes, then cover with cling film and refrigerate for at least 2 hours.

6 Finishing the dish. Pre-heat the oven to 160°C/325°F/Gas Mark 3. Pour the tomato sauce into a 20 cm (8 in) oval gratin dish and arrange the quenelles in it. Sprinkle the Gruyère on top and bake for 15 minutes, until the cheese has coloured lightly (put the dish under the grill for a few minutes if necessary).

3 Making the tomato sauce. On a low heat, in a medium saucepan, soften the onion, garlic and thyme for 2–3 minutes in the olive oil. Add the tomatoes and tomato purée and cook on a medium heat for 7–8 minutes. Add the water, season with 2 pinches of salt and a pinch of pepper and cook for 5 minutes. Taste and correct the seasoning, adding the sugar if necessary. Purée the sauce in a food processor or blender. Strain through a sieve if you want a very smooth sauce.

4 Shaping the quenelles. Divide the semolina mixture in half. With your hands, on a lightly floured work surface, roll each half into a big sausage shape, about 20 x 4 cm (8 x 1½ in). Cut each piece in half again to obtain four 10 cm (4 in) quenelles.

5 Cooking the quenelles. In a large saucepan, bring the water to simmering point. Slide the quenelles carefully into the simmering water. They will sink to the bottom but will rise to the surface when cooked; this will take 8–10 minutes. With a fish slice, lift the cooked quenelles carefully on to kitchen paper to absorb excess water.

Stuffed tomatoes

The French call tomatoes *pommes d'amour*, or 'apples of love'. They would, wouldn't they, for they bring love into every sphere of their lives – especially food, of course. Mind you, if on a summer's day you can pick, hold and smell this heavenly fruit, fleshy and scented, glowing red in its green foliage, you might begin to understand what they mean. Do not bruise your tomatoes; bring them home safely and, if necessary, let them ripen fully on your windowsill, then you might be lucky enough to enjoy the taste of real tomatoes. Needless to say, you are not likely to experience this if you buy cheap, tasteless tomatoes with flesh like cotton wool. For this dish you need proper Marmande tomatoes, grown outdoors.

serves 4
preparation time: 45 minutes
cooking time: 1 hour

4 large, ripe Marmande or beef tomatoes (organic if possible), about 200 g (7 oz) each

1 tablespoon extra-virgin olive oil

chopped fresh chives, to garnish

For the tomato sauce:

1 medium onion, finely chopped

2 garlic cloves, crushed

2 sprigs of fresh thyme

3 tablespoons olive oil

4 ripe tomatoes, chopped

100 g (4 oz) tomato purée

400 ml (14 fl oz) water

3 pinches of sugar (optional)

sea salt and freshly ground black pepper

For the stuffing:

50 g (2 oz) white onion, finely chopped

20 g (3/4 oz) unsalted butter

1 teaspoon fresh thyme leaves

1 bay leaf

100 g (4 oz) long grain rice, washed and drained

200 ml (7 fl oz) water

30 g (1 1/4 oz) carrot, very finely sliced (about 1 mm thick)

30 g (1 1/4 oz) celery, sliced 2 mm (1/12 in) thick

30 g (1 1/4 oz) courgette, sliced 2 mm (1/12 in) thick

30 g (1 1/4 oz) fresh or frozen peas

2 tablespoons whipping cream

75 g (3 oz) Gruyère cheese, finely grated

sea salt and freshly ground white pepper

1 **Making the tomato sauce.** On a low heat, in a medium saucepan, soften the onion, garlic and thyme for 2–3 minutes in the olive oil. Add the tomatoes and tomato purée and cook on a medium heat for 7–8 minutes, until the tomatoes have cooked down. Add the water, season with 2 pinches of salt and a pinch of pepper and cook for 5 minutes. Taste and correct the seasoning, adding the sugar if necessary. Purée the sauce in a food processor or blender (strain through a sieve as well if you want a very smooth sauce) and set aside.

2 **Preparing the tomatoes.** Slice about a third off the top of each tomato to make a hat; set this aside. With a spoon, scoop out the pulp and juices from the tomatoes into a bowl and set aside.

3 **Making the stuffing.** On a medium heat, in a medium saucepan, soften the onion in the butter with the thyme and bay leaf for 3 minutes, without letting it colour. Stir in the rice and cook for 1 minute, then add the water, the sliced carrot, 150 ml (1/4 pint) of the reserved tomato pulp and juice, plus 2 pinches of salt and a pinch of white pepper. Bring to the boil, then reduce the heat to a gentle simmer and cook for 5 minutes, stirring from time to time.

4 Add the celery, courgette and peas and cook for 15 minutes. Stir in the cream and grated cheese. Taste and correct the seasoning if necessary.

5 **Stuffing and cooking the tomatoes.** Pre-heat the oven to 180°C/350°F/Gas Mark 4. Divide the rice stuffing between the tomatoes and top each of them with a tomato 'hat'. Place them in a baking dish, drizzle with the extra-virgin olive oil and bake for 20 minutes. To serve, reheat the tomato sauce and pour it into the baking dish around the stuffed tomatoes, or you can serve directly on individual plates. Garnish with chopped chives.

Petits pois à la française

Freshly picked young peas are always the best but frozen peas are excellent, too. I must say that Bird's Eye were the best we tried for this recipe because they are harvested very young and frozen within 24 hours, so retain optimum flavour and freshness.

If you prefer, you could omit the bacon and stir in some parsley and chervil at the end instead to create a delicious vegetarian alternative.

serves 4
preparation time: 15 minutes
cooking time: 25 minutes

20 baby onions, peeled

50 g (2 oz) smoked streaky bacon, rind removed, cut into lardons (little strips) 3 mm (1/8 in) thick

25 g (1 oz) unsalted butter

200 ml (7 fl oz) water

3 pinches of sugar

400 g (14 oz) shelled young fresh peas or frozen peas

1 Webb's lettuce or other soft lettuce, leaves separated

sea salt and freshly ground black pepper

1 **Cooking the onions and bacon.** On a low heat, in a small saucepan, soften the baby onions and bacon lardons in the butter for 2–3 minutes, without colouring.

2 Add the water, sugar, 5 pinches of salt and a pinch of black pepper and bring to the boil. Cover with a lid and reduce the heat to just below a simmer (with bubbles just breaking the surface). Cook for 15–20 minutes, until the onions are translucent, soft and melting but still retain some texture.

3 **Cooking the peas.** Remove the lid, turn the heat to high and add the peas and lettuce leaves. Stir, then cover again and cook for 1–2 minutes, until the peas are tender. Taste and correct the seasoning if required.

Gratin dauphinois

Seriously satisfying…layers of potato cooked in a rich garlic cream with Gruyère cheese. This dish goes best with roast meat, particularly beef. The potato variety is important. I find that Desiree and Belle de Fontenay work best, and both are usually available in supermarkets. The gratin can be cooked an hour or so before the meal and then reheated 20 minutes before serving.

serves 4
preparation time: 15 minutes
cooking time: 50 minutes

4 medium potatoes (Desiree or Belle de Fontenay), weighing about 450 g (1 lb) in total

300 ml (1/2 pint) full-fat milk

100 ml (31/2 fl oz) double cream

8 gratings of nutmeg

100 g (4 oz) Gruyère cheese, grated

1/2 garlic clove, peeled

salt and freshly ground black or white pepper

1 **Preparing the potatoes.** Preheat the oven to 120°C/250°F/Gas Mark 1/2. Peel the potatoes and slice them 2 mm (1/12 in) thick – a mandoline will make the job easier (see page 19). Do not wash the potato slices, as you need to keep the starch in them to help thicken the cream.

2 On a medium heat, in a medium saucepan, bring the milk and cream to the boil. Add the sliced potatoes and stir to coat them with the cream. Season with the nutmeg, 5 pinches of salt and 2 pinches of pepper.

3 Lower the heat and simmer for 8–10 minutes, stirring every 2 minutes to prevent the mixture sticking to the base of the pan and to distribute the heat throughout the potatoes. Stir in the grated cheese and then remove the pan from the heat.

4 **Baking the gratin.** Rub a 20 cm (8 in) gratin dish with the garlic. With a spatula, spread the potato mixture out evenly in the dish. Place in the oven and bake for 35 minutes; there should be tiny bubbles on the surface of the dish. The gratin is cooked when the tip of a sharp knife cuts into it with little resistance (you shouldn't feel the layers). To brown the top, place under a hot grill for 2–3 minutes. Leave to rest for 5 minutes before serving.

Potato purée

A French potato purée is so different from an English mash. One is light, with fluffy peaks, melting and completely delicious; the other is dense and heavy, folds in your stomach, and has only one purpose – to fill you up …

The variety of potato used is of the utmost importance, since it will define the taste, texture and lightness of the purée. The best potatoes to use are Desiree, Belle de Fontenay, Estima and Maris Piper. The potential variations on this dish are enormous – try adding garlic, olive oil, mustard, nutmeg, and any herbs you like.

serves 4
preparation time: 15 minutes
cooking time: 25–30 minutes

For cooking the potatoes:

1 kg (2¹/₄ lb) Desiree, Belle de Fontenay, Estima or Maris Piper potatoes, peeled and cut into quarters

2 litres (3¹/₂ pints) cold water

20 g (³/₄ oz) salt

To finish the purée:

175–200 ml (6–7 fl oz) full-fat milk, boiled

75 g (3 oz) unsalted butter, melted

sea salt and freshly ground white pepper

1 **Cooking the potatoes.** Put the potatoes, water and salt in a large saucepan and bring to the boil on a high heat. Reduce the heat so that the water is gently simmering (with bubbles just breaking the surface) and cook for 25–30 minutes, until the potatoes are soft. Do not let it boil rapidly or the potatoes will be overcooked and watery.

2 **Puréeing the potatoes.** Strain the cooked potatoes through a colander and leave for 2–3 minutes to let the excess steam escape. Pass the potatoes through a potato ricer or sieve, or mash them thoroughly with a potato masher.

3 **Finishing the purée.** Return the potato purée to the saucepan and gradually mix in the hot milk (reserve a little). Then stir in the melted butter and season with 2 pinches of salt and 2 pinches of white pepper. Taste and correct the seasoning if necessary. If the purée is too firm, thin it down with the remaining milk. You have the perfect purée when it is fluffy, forms firm peaks and melts in your mouth.

Cherry clafoutis

Clafoutis is a great family dish. Of course, my mum's recipe was the best, and it is now one of our bestsellers at the Le Petit Blanc restaurants. Everyone should know how to make this dessert. It is so easy to prepare and your children, husband, wife and friends will love you two thousand times more for it.

Put the clafoutis in the oven just before you sit down to eat your meal, then it will be at the right temperature when you serve it; just warm is best.

serves 4
preparation time: 30 minutes,
  plus 2 hours' marinating
cooking time: 30–35 minutes

For the cherries:

500 g (1 lb 2 oz) fresh
  cherries, stoned

2 tablespoons caster sugar,
  plus extra to serve

2 tablespoons kirsch (optional)

For the dish:

10 g (¼ oz) unsalted butter,
  melted

3 tablespoons caster sugar

For the batter:

100 g (4 oz) plain white flour

a pinch of salt

3 organic or free range eggs

1 organic or free range egg
  yolk

6 tablespoons caster sugar

finely grated zest of 1 lemon

6 drops of natural vanilla
  extract (optional)

150 ml (¼ pint) milk

150 ml (¼ pint) whipping
  cream

75 g (3 oz) unsalted butter

1 **Marinating the cherries.** Mix the cherries with the sugar and the kirsch, if using, and leave for 2 hours to maximize their flavour.

2 **Preparing the baking dish.** Brush the inside of a round or oval cast iron or china baking dish, 20 cm (8 in) in diameter and 5 cm (2 in) deep, with the melted butter. Sprinkle in the caster sugar and shake the dish so it coats the inside evenly. This will give the clafoutis a lovely crust during cooking. Pre-heat the oven to 180°C/350°F/Gas Mark 4.

3 Making the batter. Put the flour and salt in a mixing bowl and make a well in the centre. Add the eggs, egg yolk, sugar, lemon zest and the vanilla, if using. With a whisk, slowly incorporate the egg mixture into the flour until smooth. Whisk in the milk and cream.

4 In a small saucepan, heat the butter until it turns a pale hazelnut colour, then whisk it into the batter while still hot.

5 Finishing the clafoutis. Mix the cherries and their juices into the batter and then pour into the baking dish. Bake for 30–35 minutes, until the blade of a knife inserted into the mixture comes out completely clean. Sprinkle a little caster sugar over and serve warm.

Chocolate mousse

This is undoubtedly the best chocolate mousse I have ever eaten, and I can recommend it for every day or for any party or celebration. Do use the very best chocolate, with 70 per cent cocoa solids, and also the very best unsweetened cocoa powder, then you will have the very best chocolate experience.

serves 4

preparation time: 20 minutes, plus 2 hours' chilling

165 g (5½ oz) dark chocolate, at least 70% cocoa solids, finely chopped

25g (1 oz) unsweetened cocoa powder

10 organic or free range egg whites

25 g (1 oz) caster sugar

1 organic or free range egg yolk

1 Melting the chocolate. Place the chocolate and cocoa powder in a large bowl set over a pan of hot water and leave to melt over a low heat; do not boil the water or the chocolate will become grainy. Stir until smooth, then remove from the heat. Keep warm over the pan of water while you whisk the egg whites.

2 Whisking the egg whites. With an electric beater, whisk the egg whites and sugar for 2–3 minutes, until they form soft peaks.

3 Adding the eggs to the chocolate. Stir the egg yolk into the chocolate and cocoa mixture and immediately whisk in a quarter of the egg whites to lighten the mixture.

4 Fold in the remaining egg whites with a large spatula, ensuring that you do not over mix or the mousse will be heavy. Pour into a glass bowl or individual glasses and leave to set in the fridge for 2 hours or until required.

Crème caramel

This must be the French national dessert, enjoyed in every home, every brasserie and even many Michelin-starred restaurants. There are two points to watch when making crème caramel: first, the caramel must be allowed to turn a deep brown, almost to the point of burning – too pale and it will taste sweet with no caramel flavour; too dark and it will be bitter. Secondly, the custard mixture should be cooked until it is only just set, otherwise you will lose that magical melting-snow effect in the mouth.

serves 4
preparation time: 30 minutes
cooking time: 55–60 minutes,
  plus chilling for 2 hours or
  overnight

For the caramel:
2 tablespoons water
120 g (4¹/₂ oz) caster sugar

For the custard mixture:
500 ml (17 fl oz) full-fat milk
¹/₂ vanilla pod, split open
  lengthways and seeds
  removed (see page 16), or
  ¹/₂ teaspoon natural vanilla
  extract
2 organic or free range eggs
3 organic or free range egg
  yolks
100 g (4 oz) caster sugar

1 **Making the caramel.** Put the water in a small, heavy-based saucepan and scatter the sugar over it in an even layer. Let the sugar absorb the water for a few minutes, then place the pan on a medium heat and leave, without stirring, until the sugar has dissolved and formed a syrup.

2 Simmer until the syrup turns into a rich brown caramel (there should be a light haze and it should smell wonderful). Wrap a cloth around your hand and immediately remove the pan from the heat. Pour the caramel into 4 ramekins, about 7.5 cm (3 in) in diameter and 5 cm (2 in) deep; tilt each ramekin slightly so the caramel coats the base evenly. Transfer the ramekins to a baking tin and set aside.

3 Making the custard mixture.
Pre-heat the oven to 160°C/
325°F/Gas Mark 3. Put the
milk in a saucepan with the
vanilla pod and seeds (or
vanilla extract) and bring just
to simmering point for 3–4
minutes to allow the milk to
become infused with the
vanilla. Meanwhile, in a large
bowl, lightly whisk the eggs
and egg yolks with the sugar.
Slowly pour in the hot milk,
whisking all the time.

4 Cooking the crème caramel.
Strain the mixture through a
fine sieve into the caramel-
lined ramekins. Place the
baking tin containing the
ramekins in the oven and
carefully pour enough boiling
water into the tin to come
two-thirds of the way up the
side of the moulds.

5 Bake for 55–60 minutes, until
the crème caramels are just
set (press gently with your
finger to check). Any dip in
the centre means they are
undercooked. Remove from
the oven and leave to cool,
then chill for 2 hours (or
overnight, if more convenient). To release each crème
caramel from the dish, take a
thin, sharp knife and slide it
around the inside edge of the
ramekin, then turn it upside
down on to a serving plate
(or, more simply, serve them
in their ramekins).

Floating islands 'Maman Blanc'

A dessert from my childhood, a big treat for children and for all the grown-ups, too: real vanilla custard, topped with huge meringue islands coated with a fine layer of dark, crispy caramel. This dish used to grace every festive occasion in France. Please do not use artificial vanilla essence; instead buy plump, dark vanilla pods for the best vanilla experience.

The vanilla custard and poached meringue will taste much better if made a day in advance but the caramel coating should be added no more than an hour before serving, so it retains its crispness.

serves 4–6
preparation time: 40 minutes
cooking time: 25 minutes

For poaching the meringue:

1.25 litres (2¼ pints) full-fat milk

2 vanilla pods, split lengthways (see page 16)

For the meringue:

8 medium organic or free range egg whites

275 g (10 oz) caster sugar

For the vanilla custard:

8 medium organic or free range egg yolks

75 g (3 oz) caster sugar

milk used for poaching the meringue

For the caramel:

50 ml (2 fl oz) water

150 g (5 oz) caster sugar

1 **Infusing the milk.** Pour the milk into a large, shallow pan, about 30 cm (12 in) in diameter and 7.5 cm (3 in) deep, and bring to simmering point. Scrape the vanilla seeds into the milk with the point of a sharp knife and whisk to disperse them; add the split vanilla pods, too. Bring to the boil and reduce the heat to a slow simmer for 5 minutes to infuse the milk with the vanilla.

2 **Making the meringue.** Whisk the egg whites and sugar with an electric beater on full power for at least 10 minutes, until the mixture forms shiny, firm peaks.

3 **Poaching the meringue.** With a large spoon, carefully scoop out 4 or 6 large chunks of meringue. Poach in the gently simmering milk for 5 minutes on each side, taking great care not to damage the delicate meringue when turning it over. If the milk begins to boil and rise out of the pan, turn down the heat and gently push the meringue sideways so the build-up of heat and steam can escape. Carefully lift the poached meringue on to a baking tray and set aside. Strain the milk into a saucepan.

4 **Making the vanilla custard.** In a large bowl, whisk the egg yolks with the caster sugar, then gradually whisk in the hot milk. Pour the mixture back into the saucepan.

5 Cook over a medium heat for 4–5 minutes, until the custard begins to thicken. Stir constantly to distribute the heat and lift the spoon every 10–15 seconds to check if the sauce is thickening (when it is ready it will coat the back of the spoon). Strain immediately into a large bowl and continue stirring for 2 minutes to stop any further cooking, otherwise the custard could scramble (if this happens, don't panic; pour it immediately into a blender or food processor and blend for 30–40 seconds so it regains its consistency). Leave to cool, then chill. Pour into a large serving bowl and, with a fish slice, carefully place the poached meringues on top of the vanilla custard to create your floating dessert islands.

6 **Making the caramel.** Put the water in a small, heavy-based saucepan and scatter the sugar over it in an even layer. Let the sugar absorb the water for a few minutes, then place the pan on a medium heat and leave, without stirring, until the sugar has dissolved and formed a syrup. Simmer until it turns to a golden brown caramel. Immediately place the bottom of the saucepan in cold water to stop the caramel cooking any further.

7 Pour a fine coating of caramel over the poached meringues. Wait a few seconds until the caramel sets before serving (or leave it for up to 1 hour).

Pain perdu with warm raspberries and strawberries

Another vivid childhood memory. Pain perdu means 'lost bread' (in England it is often known as French toast), and this recipe was devised as a means of using up leftover bread. I will always remember the large earthenware bowl, full of golden liquid, in which the stale bread would soak at home. Today we are not victims of a wartime economy and have the luxury of using brioche if we prefer. The red fruits can be replaced by apples or peaches, in which case you will need to increase the cooking time by up to 5 minutes for apples or 3 minutes for peaches.

serves 4
preparation time: 20 minutes, plus 8–10 minutes' soaking
cooking time: 15 minutes

For the pain perdu:

2 large organic or free range eggs

50 g (2 oz) caster sugar

100 ml (3½ fl oz) full-fat milk

2 teaspoons rum or cognac (optional)

a few drops of best-quality vanilla extract (optional)

4 slices of bread, cut 2 cm (¾ in) thick, crusts removed, cut in half

40 g (1½ oz) unsalted butter

shredded fresh mint, to decorate

For the warm raspberries and strawberries:

2 tablespoons water

50 g (2 oz) caster sugar

25 g (1 oz) chilled unsalted butter, diced

100 g (4 oz) strawberries, cut in half (or quartered if large)

100 g (4 oz) raspberries

2 teaspoons kirsch or cognac

1 **Making the egg mixture for the pain perdu.** In a large bowl, beat the eggs with the sugar until the sugar has dissolved. Gradually mix in the milk and the rum or cognac and vanilla extract, if using.

2 **Soaking the bread.** Place the slices of bread in a large dish and pour over the egg mixture. Allow the bread to soak for 4–5 minutes, then turn the slices over and soak for a further 4–5 minutes to ensure that all the liquid is absorbed. Carefully lift the bread from the dish with a fish slice and place on a baking tray.

3 **Frying the bread.** Pre-heat the oven to 150°C/300°F/Gas Mark 2. On a medium heat, in a large frying pan, melt half the butter. When it is foaming, add 2 bread slices and fry for 2 minutes on each side. Remove from the pan and set aside. Clean the pan, return it to the heat and cook the remaining bread in the remaining butter. Place on a baking tray and leave in the oven for 5 minutes.

4 **Making a pale caramel for the fruit.** Put the water in a medium frying pan and scatter the sugar over it in an even layer. Let the sugar absorb the water for a few minutes, then place the pan on a medium heat and leave, without stirring, until the sugar has dissolved and formed a syrup. Simmer until the syrup turns into a very pale blond caramel.

5 **Cooking the fruit.** Stir the diced butter into the caramel, add the strawberries and raspberries, then the kirsch or cognac, and cook for 30 seconds to soften the fruit and create delicious juices. To serve, remove the hot slices of bread from the oven and place on 4 plates. Spoon the warm strawberries and raspberries over the bread and spoon the red fruit syrup around, then garnish with a little shredded mint.

Lemon tart

Lemon tart is a favourite dessert. Making it is quite a lengthy process but relatively simple. You could prepare double the quantity of pastry and freeze half for another dessert, if you wish.

serves 4–6
preparation time: 40 minutes, plus 1 hour's chilling
cooking time: 55 minutes

For the sweet pastry:

120 g (4¹/₂ oz) unsalted butter, at room temperature, diced

75 g (3 oz) icing sugar, sifted, plus extra for dusting

3 egg yolks

250 g (9 oz) plain flour

2 tablespoons water

For the lemon cream:

5 medium organic or free range eggs

150 g (5 oz) caster sugar

85 ml (3 fl oz) lemon juice

2 tablespoons finely grated lemon zest

150 ml (¹/₄ pint) double cream

1 **Making the sweet pastry.** In a large bowl, with a spatula or wooden spoon, mix the soft butter and icing sugar to a cream; then beat in 2 of the egg yolks.

2 Add the flour and, with your fingertips, rub the butter mixture and flour together to achieve a crumbly texture. Add the water and press the mixture together to form a ball.

3 With the palms of your hands, knead the pastry on a lightly floured work surface until it is blended (maximum 30 seconds – do not overwork the pastry or it will be hard and lose its crumbly texture). Flatten the pastry slightly with the palm of your hand, wrap in cling film and refrigerate for 30 minutes (this helps the dough lose its elasticity).

4 **Making the lemon cream.** In a large bowl, mix together the eggs, sugar, lemon juice and zest and whisk for a few seconds. Add the cream and whisk it in, then place in the fridge.

5 **Rolling out the pastry.** On a lightly floured work surface, evenly roll out the pastry into a circle 3 mm (1/8 in) thick.

6 **Lining the tart tin.** Roll the pastry over the rolling pin and unroll it over a 24 cm (9½ in) loose-bottomed tart tin. With one hand lift the pastry and with the other gently tuck it into the bottom edge of the tin so that it fits tightly. Be careful not to stretch it. Cut off excess pastry by rolling the pin over the top edge of the tin. Take a small ball of pastry and gently press it all around the base of the tart to ensure a snug fit. Prick the base of the pastry all over with a fork and refrigerate for 30 minutes (this helps prevent shrinkage during cooking). Meanwhile, pre-heat the oven to 160°C/ 325°F/Gas Mark 3.

7 Cooking the pastry. Line the pastry case with aluminium foil and fill with dried beans, pushing them against the side. Bake for 10 minutes, then remove from the oven and lift out both foil and beans. Return the tart tin to the oven and bake for a further 20 minutes. Brush the inside of the pastry with the remaining egg yolk and return to the oven for 1 minute (this creates a seal on the pastry and prevents it becoming soggy when the lemon cream is added). Turn the oven down to 140°C/275°F/Gas Mark 1.

8 Cooking the lemon tart. Pour the lemon cream mixture into a saucepan and warm it gently (this is to speed up the cooking time of the tart), being careful not to heat it too much or it will scramble. Pour the warm mixture into the pastry case and bake for 25 minutes, until barely set. Remove from the oven and leave to cool for at least 1 hour, then dredge icing sugar around the edge of the tart. Remove the tart from the tin and place on a serving plate.

Peaches poached in white wine and citrus fruits

The perfect dessert when peaches are in season; June and July are usually the best months. The finest peaches come from France and Italy. White peaches have the very best flavour and for that there is a small extra price to pay.

serves 4
preparation time: 20 minutes, plus 6 hours' chilling
cooking time: 25 minutes

8 ripe but firm peaches, white if possible

1 orange

1/2 lemon

175 g (6 oz) caster sugar

500 ml (17 fl oz) water

500 ml (17 fl oz) dry white wine

1 vanilla pod, split open lengthways and seeds removed (see page 16)

8 sprigs of spearmint

1 Preparing the fruit. Remove the stalks from the peaches. Cut the orange and lemon into fine slices about 3 mm (1/8 in) thick, leaving the rind on.

2 Arranging the fruit in the pan. Place the peaches in a large saucepan in a single layer. Add the caster sugar, water, white wine, vanilla pod and seeds. Top with the orange and lemon slices. Cut out a round of greaseproof paper the same size as the saucepan and cut a hole in the centre to allow excess steam to escape. Place it directly on top of the peaches.

3 Poaching the fruit. On a high heat, bring to the boil. Immediately reduce the heat to a gentle simmer and cook for about 20 minutes (the flesh of peaches is very delicate; if subjected to high heat, their texture will be ruined, so cook them very gently). There is an easy way to see if the peaches are cooked or not: you will notice some tiny bubbles escaping from the point where you removed the stalk; when these bubbles stop coming out, the peach is ready. Turn off the heat and leave the peaches to cool in the liquid.

4 **Adding the mint.** Chop 4 sprigs of mint and mix them into the syrup. Refrigerate for at least 6 hours and up to 24, to allow the exchange of flavours between the citrus, mint and peaches.

5 **Serving the peaches.** With a slotted spoon, transfer the peaches to a plate and carefully peel off the skin. Place the peaches, orange and lemon slices and vanilla pod in a glass serving bowl and pour the white wine and citrus syrup over (if you have too much syrup, freeze it and scrape beautiful frozen flakes of it into glasses to serve as a pre-dessert at a future meal). Arrange the remaining 4 sprigs of spearmint on top.

Tarte Tatin

This amazing, sensuous dessert was invented at the turn of the twentieth century by two elderly spinsters, the Tatin sisters – the world owes them a great deal! All the elements of pleasure are here: the dark caramel, the sweet and acid taste of the apple, the crisp pastry. Serve with the very best crème fraîche (full fat, please) or a scoop of vanilla ice-cream. Should you wish, you can cook the tart one day in advance, keep it in the tin and reheat it at 150°C/300°F/Gas Mark 2 for 20 minutes. However, the best way to eat it is an hour or so after cooking, when it is still warm.

serves 4
preparation time: 40 minutes
cooking time: 1 hour 20 minutes

For the tart:

200 g (7 oz) bought puff pastry, thawed if frozen

8 large Cox's apples, peeled, halved and cored with a melon baller

10 g (¼ oz) unsalted butter, melted

1 tablespoon caster sugar

For the caramel:

50 ml (2 fl oz) water

100 g (4 oz) caster sugar

25 g (1 oz) unsalted butter

1 **Preparing the pastry.** On a lightly floured surface, roll out the puff pastry to 2 mm (1/12 in) thick and prick it all over with a fork. Transfer to a baking tray, cover with cling film and refrigerate for 20–30 minutes to firm it up and prevent shrinkage whilst cooking. Cut out a 20 cm (8 in) circle, using a plate or cake tin as a template, prick with a fork and chill again.

2 **Making the caramel.** Put the water in a small, heavy-based saucepan and scatter the sugar over it in an even layer. Let the sugar absorb the water for a few minutes, then place the pan on a medium heat and leave, without stirring, until the sugar has dissolved and formed a syrup. Simmer until it turns to a golden brown caramel. Stir in the butter and immediately pour the caramel into an 18 cm (7 in) round baking tin, 4–5 cm (1½–2 in) deep.

3 **Filling the tin with the apples.** Pre-heat the oven to 190°C/375°F/Gas Mark 5. Arrange 12 apple halves upright around the edge of the tin to complete a full circle. In the middle sit half an apple, flat-side up, then top with another half apple. Cut the remaining apple into slices and wedge them into the empty spaces. You need to pack tight as many apple pieces as you can into the tin, so that you leave as little space as possible; this will give the perfect density and the perfect slice. Brush the melted butter over the apples and sprinkle the caster sugar over the top.

4 **Baking the tart.** Place the tin in the oven and bake for 35 minutes, until the apples are partly cooked. Remove from the oven, place the puff pastry circle on top of the hot apples and tuck the edge of the pastry inside the tin. Cook for a further 30 minutes, until the pastry is golden brown. Place the tarte Tatin next to an open window, if possible, and leave for 1–2 hours, until barely warm.

5 **Unmoulding the tart.** Slide the blade of a sharp knife full circle inside the tin to release the tarte Tatin. Place a large dinner plate over the tart and, holding both tin and plate together, turn it upside down, shaking it gently sideways to release the tart on to the plate.

Riz au lait

Riz au lait is what the British call rice pudding. It is a timeless classic dish from French home cooking, both for children and adults. Every mother has her own recipe, which she hands down through her family, and of course hers is always the best. I had a serious 'argument' with my chef pâtissier, M. Benoit, whose mother's recipe was entirely different from mine, about whose recipe was best, and I won – sorry, my mother won!

You can bake the rice pudding 1–2 hours in advance and serve it warm rather than hot. It can be served with poached pears or peaches in vanilla.

serves 4
preparation time: 10 minutes
cooking time: 1 hour

850 ml (28 fl oz) full-fat milk

50 g (2 oz) caster sugar

1 vanilla pod, split length-ways and seeds scraped out (see page 16), or a few drops of natural vanilla extract

75 g (3 oz) short grain (pud-ding) rice, washed in cold water and drained

caster sugar or icing sugar for sprinkling

2 Cooking the rice. Pre-heat the oven to 150°C/300°F/Gas Mark 2. Add the rice to the milk and return to a medium boil. On a medium-high heat, cook the rice for 30 minutes, stirring every 5 minutes. Towards the end of the cooking, as the milk becomes more condensed and the consistency thickens, stir every 2 minutes or so to prevent the rice sticking to the bottom of the saucepan.

1 Boiling the milk, sugar and vanilla. On a medium heat, in a medium saucepan, bring the milk, sugar, vanilla pod and seeds (or vanilla extract) to the boil.

3 **Baking the rice pudding.** Pour the rice into a shallow baking dish, about 24 cm (9½ in) in diameter, and bake in the oven for 30 minutes.

4 **Caramelizing the pudding.** Pre-heat the grill. Remove the pudding from the oven and sprinkle caster or icing sugar over the top so it is completely covered. Caramelize under a hot grill for 1 minute.

Galette des rois

This dessert is served just once a year, on 6 January (Epiphany), and every child in France waits for it eagerly. It is to honour the kings who travelled hundreds of miles to welcome our Saviour … actually this is a load of old baloney, as it was probably invented by an opportunistic pâtissier, who obviously saw the chance for a huge market. It makes a marvellous party dessert, as traditionally two little figurines can be hidden in the almond cream. The ones who find them become king and queen for the day and, of course, have all of their wishes granted. Two crowns would be perfectly fitting for the winners.

serves 4

preparation time: 30 minutes, plus 1 hour 40 minutes' chilling

cooking time: 45 minutes

For the puff pastry:

500 g (1 lb 2 oz) bought puff pastry

1 large egg yolk, beaten with 1 teaspoon water, to glaze

For the almond cream:

75 g (3 oz) soft unsalted butter

75 g (3 oz) icing sugar

75 g (3 oz) ground almonds

1 large organic or free range egg

1 large organic or free range egg yolk

1 tablespoon dark rum or cognac

1 Preparing the pastry. On a lightly floured work surface, roll out the puff pastry into a 50 x 30 cm (20 x 12 in) rectangle, 2 mm (1/12 in) thick. Transfer to a baking tray, cover with cling film and place in the fridge for 30 minutes to firm up the pastry and prevent shrinkage whilst cooking. Cut out two 20 cm (8 in) circles, using a plate or cake tin as a template, and refrigerate again for at least 30 minutes.

2 Making the almond cream. In a large bowl, with a whisk, mix the soft butter to a cream with the icing sugar. Gradually mix in the ground almonds, then the egg, egg yolk and rum or cognac. Mix until smooth, then set aside in the fridge for 30 minutes.

3 Assembling the galette.

Pre-heat the oven to 180°C/ 350°F/Gas Mark 4. Place one disc of pastry on a baking sheet lined with baking parchment. Spoon the almond cream into the centre. With a palette knife, spread the cream into an even circle, leaving a 4 cm (1½ in) border all round. Brush a little of the beaten glaze over the border and carefully drape the other circle of pastry neatly on top, pressing gently on the edge to seal it. With the back of a knife, score the outside edge of the pastry all around (this will completely seal the 2 rounds of pastry and also make an attractive presentation).

4 Glazing, scoring and baking the galette.

Brush the top of the galette with the beaten egg yolk and water mixture, then refrigerate for 10 minutes, so it has time to dry; repeat again to give a richer colour (ensure that you do not brush egg yolk on the outside edge of the galette or it will prevent the puff pastry rising). Now you can use your artistic flair. With the side of a fork or knife, starting from the centre of the galette, score a spiral to the edge of the pastry. Repeat this to achieve an attractive design (if you feel unsure, you could simply make criss-cross lines). Bake in the oven for 45 minutes, until golden brown.

Menus

Good food and wine are at last very much part of our everyday lives. In the UK we now entertain more than our French and Italian counterparts … oh, *mon dieu*! In this book I have chosen the recipes that are not only the most delicious but are also easily recreated in your own home. The simple act of cooking can turn into a rewarding experience for both yourself and your guests. Every cook knows that.

Interestingly enough, most of our celebrations take place around the table. I have never yet seen a takeaway served at a wedding, nor a couple sharing a romantic moment with a burger, nor a tin of baked beans opened on a first date (or only under duress!). No. One makes an effort. Food has always been a strong medium for showing friendship, love and care. Each of the following menus has been chosen to fit a particular occasion and many of them can be prepared in advance. If necessary, increase or decrease the quantities in the recipes to serve the required number of people.

Elegant Dinner Party

Here you need solid organisation. Keep the number of your guests up to six and always choose simple but delicious dishes, some of which can be prepared in advance. All the dishes here answer the last of these criteria. All you will have to do is pour the wine and enjoy that moment of triumph.

Chicken Liver Parfait

Duck Leg Confit with Flageolet Beans

Tarte Tatin

Easy Dinner Party

For me, time is a luxury, so I must confess I often create this type of dinner party. All the ingredients can be put together in very little time. Add the dressing to the salad at the last moment, so the leaves do not become wilted. Both the ratatouille and tomato coulis can be made well in advance, leaving just the sea bream fillets to cook. The clafoutis can be made a few hours in advance and reheated in a warm oven for 10–15 minutes before serving.

Roquefort, Walnut and Chicory Salad

Pan-fried Fillet of Sea Bream with Ratatouille and Tomato Coulis

Cherry Clafoutis

Romantic Dinner

This menu allows you to display both your culinary skills and your speed, by cooking the mussels in front of your loved one. The lamb can be cooked rare 1–2 hours in advance and the peaches can be prepared the day before. This menu will not only dazzle your loved one but will allow you to be with him or her.

Moules Marinière

Provençal Rack of Lamb with Crushed Peas

Gratin Dauphinois

Peaches Poached in White Wine and Citrus Fruits

Romantic Vegetarian Dinner

These are three of my favourite dishes, which will grace any table, including that of carnivores. Furthermore, with the artichokes, tomatoes and chocolate, you have all the elements for food associated with romance.

Poached Artichokes with Mustard Vinaigrette

Stuffed Tomatoes

Chocolate Mousse

Healthy Family Meal

This could be the ideal meal for my own family gathering. All are simple dishes, with typical French character. I particularly love the poached peaches at the end. It certainly fits my definition of good nutrition: wonderful ingredients that are simply cooked and taste delicious.

Maman Blanc's Vegetable and Chervil Soup

Chicken Fricassée with Vinegar and Herbs

Petits Pois à la Française

Peaches Poached in White Wine and Citrus Fruits

Family Meal

I wish I could sit down with you for this meal as I have shared it so many times with my parents in my native Franche-Comté. This simple, wholesome menu demonstrates the appeal of French cuisine. More please!

Gruyère, Ham and Mushroom Salad with Cream and Mustard Dressing

Pot-au-Feu of Braised Pork Belly

Riz au Lait

Index